Study Guide

Macroeconomics

Study Guide

Robin Bade
University of Western Ontario

Macroeconomics

MICHAEL PARKIN

Prentice-Hall, Inc., Englewood Cliffs, New Jersey 07632

Editorial/production supervision: Suzette Walker
Cover design: Ben Santora
Manufacturing buyer: Ed O'Dougherty

Printed in the United States of America

10 9 8 7 6 5 4 3 2

ISBN 0-13-542457-7

Prentice-Hall International, Inc., London
Prentice-Hall of Australia Pty. Limited, Sydney
Editora Prentice-Hall do Brasil, Ltda., Rio de Janeiro
Prentice-Hall Canada Inc., Toronto
Prentice-Hall of India Private Limited, New Delhi
Prentice-Hall of Japan, Inc., Tokyo
Prentice-Hall of Southeast Asia Pte. Ltd., Singapore
Whitehall Books Limited, Wellington, New Zealand

CONTENTS

Preface

This Study Guide provides a comprehensive set of questions (and answers) that supplement Michael Parkin's Macroeconomics. Five types of questions are provided: Multiple choice; true or false; fill in the blanks; problems; and "projects". The Guide also provides a brief statement of the objectives and a summary of each chapter in Macroeconomics. These are taken straight from the original book--reflecting my judgment that the statements of objectives and chapter summaries cannot (easily) be improved upon. They are reproduced here to provide the user of the Guide with a fully self-contained tool for review.

The Guide will be found most useful by the reader of Macroeconomics who has studied the content of a given chapter, who has worked the questions presented at the end of the chapter and who is looking for reinforcement of what has been studied but perhaps not fully digested. The Guide will also be useful to students seeking a different style of question to that presented in Macroeconomics.

Aside from being used in this way, some students may find it helpful to use the questions in the Guide as mock exams.

Answers are supplied at the end of each chapter but the reasons are not. You will usually be able to find the reasoning in Macroeconomics.

Some chapters of Macroeconomics lend themselves naturally to one type of question and some to another. I have allowed the subject matter to dictate the extent to which each type of question is used in a given chapter and have made no attempt at evenness on this score.

The "projects" are altogether different in style and intent from the other four categories of questions. The projects will take varying amounts of time to complete but are, in all cases, time consuming ventures. You may find it possible to use some of the ideas presented in the projects as the basis for a term paper or an essay. Also instructors may assign these projects in that role.

I am grateful to successive generations of students at the University of Western Ontario whose problems with, and criticisms of, Macroeconomics have helped and guided me in the construction of this Guide. I am also indebted to Yvonne Adams, Brenda Campbell, Leslie Farrant and Marg Gower for a speedy and incredibly accurate typing job in providing the camera ready copy of this Guide, and to Ann Parkin and Diane Dobell for careful proofreading.

Finally, I wish to express my gratitude to Michael Parkin for much help, encouragement as well as for many of the questions which appear in this Guide.

Robin Bade
London, Ontario

CHAPTER 1

MACROECONOMIC QUESTIONS

After completing your study of this chapter you will:

(a) Know the questions that macroeconomics seeks to answer.
(b) Know the macroeconomic policy issues on which economists disagree.
(c) Know the views of the leading "schools of thought".

Chapter Summary

A. Macroeconomic Questions

There are six questions in macroeconomics. They are, what determines:

(i) The rate of inflation?
(ii) The unemployment rate?
(iii) The level of real national income?
(iv) The rate of interest?
(v) The balance of payments?
(vi) The foreign exchange rate?

B. Macroeconomic Policy Issues

There are two major disagreements amongst economists concerning macroeconomic policy. One concerns whether policy should use global instruments or whether it should involve detailed intervention in individual markets. The other concerns whether policy should be governed by fixed rules or whether it should be varied from time to time at the discretion of the government in the light of current economic conditions.

C. Leading Schools of Thought

There are two major schools of thought--i) monetarists who advocate global instrument setting under fixed rules, and ii) Keynesians who advocate detailed intervention in a large number of individual markets with discretion to vary that intervention from time to time.

Multiple Choice

1. Macroeconomics:

   a. is concerned with all the socially important economic issues
   b. deals with all the politically relevant aspects of economics
   c. is that part of economics that seeks to understand why the rate of inflation fluctuates
   d. is the science of prices

2. Macroeconomics:

a. seeks to understand the problems of the unemployed
b. seeks to analyze the social consequences of unemployment
c. is concerned with the problems posed by unemployment for family life
d. seeks to understand why the unemployment rate fluctuates

3. Macroeconomics:

a. analyzes the factors that determine the level of real national income
b. studies the reasons why the incomes of farmers and fishermen are lower than those of industrial workers
c. explains the income differentials between developed and less-developed countries
d. analyzes the effects of pollution taxes on firms on the overall level of pollution

4. Macroeconomics:

a. explains why first-time home buyers have to pay a higher rate of interest (on their mortgage) than the rate of interest that has to be paid by the U.S. Federal Government
b. seeks to understand what determines movements in the average level of interest rates
c. shows that the payment of interest in excess of 15% is unjust
d. shows that in times of inflation lenders exploit borrowers and obtain an unfair rate of interest

5. Macroeconomics:

a. explains why Japanese car imports are damaging the economic life of the United States
b. proves that free trade between Canada and the United States would be beneficial
c. studies the effects of tariffs on imported manufactures
d. studies the factors determining a country's overall balance of payments

6. Macroeconomics:

a. studies the forces determining the rate of exchange between the pound sterling and U.S. dollar
b. proves that an exchange rate of $2.03 for the pound sterling against the U.S. dollar is too low
c. explains why the Canadian dollar will, on the average, always return to parity with the U.S. dollar
d. shows that fluctuations in foreign exchange rates are caused by foreign investment flows

7. a. Macroeconomists disagree with each other on policy issues because there simply does not exist a science of macroeconomics
   b. Some macroeconomists believe that policy should use a small number of aggregate or global instruments and others believe that policy should take the form of detailed intervention in many individual markets
   c. There are no disagreements concerning policy amongst macroeconomists
   d. Macroeconomics is entirely political and the lines of disagreement amongst macroeconomists are identical to the lines of disagreement on broader political matters

8. a. All economists agree that policy rules are required--they disagree on which rules
   b. Macroeconomics shows why policy discretion is always better than pursuing policy rules
   c. Some macroeconomists believe that policy should take the form of announcing and adhering to fixed rules; whereas, others believe that policy should be varied from time to time at the discretion of the government in the light of current economic conditions
   d. All economists agree that policy should be adjusted in light of current economic conditions

9. a. The leading school of thought in macroeconomics is monetarism
   b. The leading school of thought in macroeconomics is Keynesianism
   c. Keynesians and monetarists agree on all essential matters
   d. There are two broad schools of thought, Keynesians who advocate detailed discretionary intervention and monetarists who advocate the setting of a small number of global policy rules

True or False

1. Inflation is a modern problem. The ancient world knew nothing but price stability.

2. Unemployment was only important in the 1930s. Neither before nor since then has there been a serious unemployment problem.

3. Since real national income grows on the average each and every year, fluctuations in the level of real national income are of no concern.

4. There are, in a modern economy, many different rates of interest. This makes it impossible for macroeconomics to study the factors that determine interest rates.

5. A country's balance of payments is determined by whether or not its car workers are competitive. It is not a macroeconomic issue.

6. The factors that determine the rate of exchange between one currency and another must be largely psychological and therefore not amenable to study by economists.

7. Macroeconomics explains why governments can and should take actions designed to influence key economic variables such as inflation and unemployment. Macroeconomists disagree amongst themselves on whether government policy should be directed at influencing the values of a small number of aggregate variables or at directly controlling the prices of, or other terms concerning the exchange of a large number of specific goods and services. Although some macroeconomists advocate that governments should be bound by a set of rules such a position is impossible to enforce since governments are the ultimate sovereign powers. To advocate policy rules is foolish for the government always has better judgment than private individuals concerning the best interests of individuals.

8. Monetarists advocate budget cutting as a key to macroeconomic success.

9. Keynesians believe that they can forecast the near future of the economy much more accurately than monetarists believe.

Fill in the Blanks

1. Macroeconomics seeks to understand the forces that influence six variables which are:

(i) ______________________ (ii) ______________________

(iii) ______________________ (iv) ______________________

(v) ______________________ (vi) ______________________

2. There are two macroeconomic policy disagreements amongst economists. The first is: should macroeconomic policy be ____________ or ____________? The second disagreement is: should policy be ____________ or ____________?

3. Broadly speaking, economists fall into two schools of thought on macroeconomic policy. One group is identified by the label ____________ and the other by the label ____________.

4. A ____________ is a macroeconomist who believes that the government should have policies towards a limited number of global macroeconomic variables and that fixed rules for the behavior of these variables should be adopted. A ______________ is an economist who advocates detailed intervention to "fine tune" the economy in the neighborhood of full employment and low inflation.

Answers

Multiple Choice: 1 c 2 d 3 a 4 b 5 d 6 a 7 b 8 c 9 d
True or False: 1 F 2 F 3 F 4 F 5F 6 F 7 F 8 F 9 T
Fill in the Blanks:
1. inflation, unemployment, real income, interest rate, balance of payments, foreign exchange rate
2. detailed, global, discretionary, rule-governed
3. monetarists, Keynesian
4. monetarist, Keynesian

CHAPTER 2

U.S. MACROECONOMIC HISTORY SINCE 1900

When you have completed your study of this chapter you will:

(a) Know the main features of the evolution of the key macroeconomic variables since 1900; these include inflation, unemployment, real income, interest rates, balance of payments, and the exchange rate.
(b) Know the main macroeconomic characteristics of each decade since 1900.
(c) Sharpen your focus on the questions that macroeconomics seeks to answer.

Chapter Summary

A. Evolution of Macroeconomic Variables

The main feature of inflation has been a distinctly rising trend. There have also been clear but irregular cycles. Inflation was more erratic in the years before the Second World War and in the late 1970s than at other times. There has been a tendency for inflation rates to be higher during war years than in peacetime, although the period since the middle 1970s is an important exception to this. The greatest deflation (falling prices) occurred during the Great Depression years of 1929-1933.

Unemployment was at its worst during the Great Depression and in the years following, up to the beginning of the Second World War. There has been a distinct tendency for unemployment to rise in the postwar years. There are clear though irregular cycles in the rate of unemployment, and like inflation, these cycles are more pronounced in the years before the Second World War.

Real income growth has averaged just over 3% per annum in the period since 1900, although the trend growth rate after 1946 was some 1% per annum greater than it had been before that date. There is considerable random fluctuation in the growth rate of real income. The highest growth rates were achieved during the Second World War and the lowest during the Great Depression.

Interest rates remained remarkably steady until the Great Depression years but then fell and remained low throughout the Second World War. In the period since then, interest rates have increased and in the most recent years, dramatically so. Long-term interest rates fluctuate much less than short-term rates. Distinct cycles are visible in the short-term rates, although only slightly so in the long-term rates.

The balance of payments has, on the average, been in surplus, although the 1950s and 1960s were years of sustained deficit.

The foreign exchange rate, measured as the number of U.S. dollars required to buy one pound sterling, shows that the U.S. dollar has tended to increase in value over the long run. During the most recent period of floating exchange rates, there have been sizable fluctuations in the foreign exchange values of the U.S. dollar.

B. Decade Summaries

The averages of the macroeconomic variables in each decade of this century are set out in Table 2.1 of the textbook (page 21) and should be studied carefully. The first decade was one of macroeconomic stability with low inflation, low unemployment, high real income growth, moderate interest rates, and a modest balance of payments surplus. The decade of the teens was dominated by World War I and experienced a long burst of inflation. The 1920s were dominated by falling prices, although in all other respects, this was a fairly average period. The Great Depression was the dominant influence of the 1930s, with output falling below trend and unemployment reaching unprecedented heights. The balance of payments moved into a massive surplus during this decade. The 1940s were dominated by World War II and a return to strong inflation. The 1950s and the 1960s were decades, much like the first decade of the century. Inflation was moderate, unemployment low, real income growth strong, and interest rates steady. Through these two decades, the United States had a balance of payments deficit. The 1970s was a decade of macroeconomic problems in most dimensions: Inflation, unemployment, and interest rates all rose; output growth fell; and foreign exchange rates fluctuated markedly. As the 1980s opened, all these problems remained.

C. Questions

Why is there such variation in our inflation experience? Can we control inflation?

Why was unemployment so high and for so long in the 1930s and why is unemployment so high today?

Why does real income grow in a cyclical but erratic fashion?

Why are long-term interest rate movements relatively smooth? Why do short-term interest rates fluctuate more markedly than long-term rates?

Why has the U.S. balance of payments usually been in surplus? Why has the foreign exchange value of the U.S. dollar increased over this century?

Multiple Choice

1. a. The period of greatest price stability in the United States occurred in the 1920s and 1930s
   b. U.S. inflation has never been worse than it was from 1980 to 1982
   c. U.S. inflation has been on a rising trend over the last 80 years
   d. The three measures of inflation in the United States--the Consumer Price Index, the Personal Consumption Deflator and the GNP Deflator--tell completely different stories about U.S. inflation

2. a. There are no cycles in unemployment
   b. U.S. unemployment has been on a distinctly rising trend since 1950
   c. The worse unemployment experience in the United States since 1900 was in 1981 when its rate reached 7.6%
   d. Unemployment in the United States averaged less in the 1960s than it had done in the 1950s

3. a. Real income growth is highly predictable
   b. Real income growth fluctuates but never becomes negative--that is, real income never falls
   c. Fluctuations in real income were more volatile in the 1930s than they have been since
   d. The trend growth rate of real income has declined over the last 80 years

4. a. Real income was below trend every year from 1975 to 1981
   b. Real income never moves more than 5% above or below its trend level
   c. Aside from the Great Depression years (1930-33) real income has never been below trend
   d. Real income deviated from trend by more during the years of World War II than at any other time since 1900

5. a. Interest rates are the most volatile and unpredictable of all the macroeconomic variables
   b. Long-term interest rates were at their lowest in 1946
   c. Short-term interest rates are always less than long-term rates
   d. Interest rates were at their highest during the Great Depression years

6. a. The United States has never had a balance of payments surplus
   b. The U.S. balance of payments deficit has become a more serious problem each and every year and especially so since 1970
   c. The U.S. balance of payments surplus has become larger in the 1980s
   d. The biggest deficit in the U.S. balance of payments occurred during World War II

7. a. The U.S. dollar was at its lowest value ever against the pound sterling during World War II
   b. The value of the U.S. dollar has always been determined in the foreign exchange market
   c. The value of the U.S. dollar increased over this century
   d. The U.S. dollar has never been worth less than the pound sterling

8. a. In 1980, the values of all the macroeconomic variables were worse than they had been on the average in any other decade since the 1920s
   b. Bad though economic conditions were in 1980, they did not approach the severity of the Great Depression years of the 1930s
   c. The 1960s and the 1920s were the two most similar decades in terms of inflation, unemployment, real income growth, long-term interest rates, the balance of payments, and the exchange rate
   d. The last 80 years of U.S. macroeconomic history is a story of gradual solid progress and improvement

True or False

1. Inflation is a completely ambiguous concept. There are simply too many alternative measures of its rate and they conflict with each other too much.

2. Prices only fall in conditions of great depression.

3. Since World War II unemployment has been a persistently worsening problem.

4. Fluctuations in unemployment have become more pronounced.

5. Real income growth is highly erratic but has been less so in the period since 1950 than it was in the inter-war years.

6. Aside from the 1920s and 1930s real income has rarely deviated from trend by more than 5%.

7. Since 1920, long-term interest rates have followed a U-shaped path with a trough in the 1940s.

8. Short-term interest rates are more volatile than long-term rates but they have the same cyclical pattern.

9. The balance of payments, though sometimes in deficit, has more often been in surplus.

10. The pound sterling has been pegged against the U.S. dollar for longer periods than it has been allowed to fluctuate freely.

Fill in the Blanks

1. The average inflation rate in the United States between 1900 and 1981 was ______% and it ranged from a low of ______% in the decade of the ______ to a high of ______% in the decade of the ______.

2. The longest burst of two digit inflation, as measured by the GNP deflator, occurred between the years ______________.

3. Unemployment has ranged from a high value of ______% in ______ to a low value of ______% in ______. Since 1950 unemployment has been on a ____________ trend. The average unemployment rate between 1900 and 1981 was ______%. The most striking feature about the behavior of unemployment in the United States in this century is its ____________ ______ level from 1931 through to ____________. This was a decade in which the unemployment rate did not fall below ______%. These were the years of the Great Depression and its aftermath.

4. The average growth rate of real income between 1901 and 1981 was ______%. The decade showing the strongest average growth rate was ______. Fluctuations in the growth rate have become ______ erratic in the period since World War II as compared with those in the inter-war years. The highest growth rate of real income, ______%, occurred in the year ______ and the lowest growth rate, ______%, occurred in the year ______.

5. The largest deviation of real income above trend was in the year ______ and below trend in the year ______.

6. Long-term interest rates ____________ between 1920 and 1946 and thereafter, ______. They reached their __________ level in the 1980s. Short-term interest rates are ____________ volatile than long-term rates but follow a very similar ____________ pattern.

7. The balance of payments measures net ____________ to or ____________ from the rest of the world by U.S. residents in aggregate. If, in their economic relations with the rest of the world, aggregate U.S. sales of goods and services plus borrowing exceeds U.S. purchases of goods and services plus lending, then the balance of payments will be in ____________. The reverse situation, in which U.S. residents' sales of goods and services plus borrowing is less than their purchases of goods and services plus lending, is referred to as a ____________. The U.S. balance of payments has usually been in ____________. The U.S. balance of payments has become especially volatile since __________.

8. The U.S. dollar has usually been worth ______ than the pound sterling. The value of the U.S. dollar has gradually ____________ since 1900. The average exchange rate ($ per £) over the period 1900 to 1981 was ________.

9. The decade of the 1930s was dominated by the ______ ____________.

10. The longest period of sustained macroeconomic progress occurred in the two decades of the ________ and ________.

Project

How Different is the United States?

It is of major interest and importance to compare U.S. macroeconomic performance with that of other major countries. To undertake a systematic comparison of all dimensions of performance would be a massive undertaking. You may, however, find it interesting to compare U.S. macroeconomic performance in the period since 1970 with the performance of Canada and Japan, two of the leading trading partners of the United States. The following table provides the data for inflation (of CPI), unemployment, real income growth, and short-term interest rates for these other two countries.

1. Draw graphs similar to frame (b) of Figure 2.1, Figure 2.2, frame (c) of Figure 2.3, and Figure 2.5 in the textbook showing the behavior of inflation (of CPI), unemployment, real income growth, and short-term interest rates for the three countries, United States, Canada and Japan. Use either a different color or a different form of line (continuous, dotted, or dashed) to distinguish the three countries.

2. Write a brief narrative for each of the other two countries along the lines of that presented in Chapter 2 of the textbook (pages 11-18).

3. Write a brief comparison of the performance of the U.S. economy with the performance of each of Canada and Japan.

Year	Inflation		Unemployment		Real Income Growth		Short-term Interest Rate	
	Canada	Japan	Canada	Japan	Canada	Japan	Canada	Japan
1970	3.3	7.6	5.7	1.1	2.5	9.9	7.3	8.3
1971	2.9	10.9	6.2	1.2	6.9	7.3	4.5	6.4
1972	4.8	11.7	6.2	1.4	6.1	9.1	5.1	4.7
1973	7.6	24.4	5.5	1.3	7.5	10.0	7.5	7.2
1974	10.9	11.8	5.3	1.4	3.6	-0.5	10.5	12.5
1975	10.8	9.3	6.9	1.9	1.2	1.4	7.9	10.7
1976	7.5	8.0	7.1	2.0	5.5	5.3	9.2	7.0
1977	8.0	3.8	8.1	2.0	2.1	5.3	7.5	5.7
1978	8.9	3.6	8.4	2.2	3.6	5.1	8.5	4.4
1979	9.1	8.0	7.5	2.1	2.9	5.2	11.8	5.9
1980	10.2	4.9	7.5	2.0	0.5	4.8	12.9	10.9
1981	12.5	2.7	7.6	2.2	3.1	4.0	18.3	7.4
1982	10.8	2.7	11.0	2.4	-4.8	3.3	14.2	6.9

SOURCES: Canada: Department of Finance, Economic Review, April 1983, pp. 125, 162, 174. Bank of Canada Review, March 1984, Table 20, Series B14017. Japan: Economic Statistics Annual (a) 1982, pp. 293, 323, 335; (b) 1979 pp. 291, 313, 337; and (c) 1977 p. 323, International Financial Statistics March 1984, pp. 264-5 and International Financial Statistics Yearbook, 1982, p. 273.

Answers

Multiple Choice: 1 c 2 b 3 c 4 a 5 b 6 c 7 c 8 b

True or False: 1 F 2 F 3 T 4 F 5 T 6 F 7 T 8 T 9 T 10 T

Fill in the Blanks:

1. 2.9, -1.7, 1930s, 7.5, 1970s
2. 1916-1918
3. 24.1, 1932, 1.2, 1944, rising, 6.7, persistently high, 1940, 14
4. 3.1, 1940s, less, 15.2, 1941, -14.9, 1932
5. 1944, 1933
6. fell, rose, highest, more cyclical
7. payments, receipts, surplus, deficit, surplus, 1980
8. less, risen, 3.78
9. high unemployment
10. 1950s, 1960s

CHAPTER 3

AGGREGATE INCOME ACCOUNTING

The second part of this textbook deals with the measurement of macroeconomic activity. Before beginning to study this part, you should be sure that you are familiar with:

(i) The questions that macroeconomics seeks to answer.
(ii) The main facts about the evolution of the key macroeconomic variables in the United States since 1900.

When you have completed your study of this chapter you will:

(a) Understand the distinction between flows and stocks.
(b) Know the definitions of: output (product), income and expenditure; domestic and national; gross and net; market price and factor cost; and nominal and real.
(c) Understand the concepts of aggregate output (product), income, and expenditure.
(d) Know how aggregate income is measured, using: the expenditure approach, the factor incomes approach, and the output approach.
(e) Know how aggregate income in constant dollars (real) is measured.
(f) Know how to read the national income and expenditure accounts of the United States.

Chapter Summary

A. Flows and Stocks

A flow is a rate per unit of time such as income per annum or expenditure per month. A stock is the value of a variable at a point in time such as the amount of money you have in the bank on a particular day.

B. Some Frequently Used Terms

1. Output (product), income and expenditure:

- Output (or product) is the value of the goods and services produced in the economy.

- Income is the sum of all the incomes earned in producing the output of the economy.

- Expenditure is the sum of all expenditures on final goods and services in the economy.

2. Domestic and national:

- Domestic refers to an aggregation of economic activity taking place in a particular country.

- National refers to an aggregation of the economic activity of all residents of a country no matter in which country the activity takes place.

3. Gross and net:

- Gross is before deducting the depreciation of assets.

- Net is after deducting the depreciation of assets.

4. Market price and factor cost:

- Market price valuations are based on the prices paid by consumers and include taxes on expenditure and are net of any subsidies.

- Factor cost valuations are based on the amounts paid to the factors of production, including profits, and exclude taxes on expenditures and are gross of subsidies.

5. Nominal and real:

- Nominal valuations use prices of goods or factors of production prevailing in the current period to value the current period's output or expenditure.

- Real valuations use prices of goods or factors of production which prevailed in a base period to value the current period's output or expenditure.

C. Aggregate Output (Product), Income, and Expenditure

Aggregate output (or product) is the value of all the goods and services produced in the economy. Aggregate income is the sum of all the incomes of all the individuals in the economy. Aggregate expenditure is the sum of all the expenditures on final goods and services produced by the economy. The values of aggregate output, income, and expenditure are equal to each other.

D. Measuring Aggregate Income

The expenditure approach to aggregate income measurement samples the expenditures of households, firms, government and foreigners and makes an estimate of the sum of those expenditures. From the fact that income, expenditure and output are equal to each other, this estimate of expenditure is also an estimate of income and output.

The factor incomes approach measures the incomes of individuals and from this forms an estimate of aggregate income. From the conceptual equality of income, expenditure, and output, this provides an alternative estimate of aggregate expenditure and output as well as income.

The output approach samples the production of individual firms and from this forms an estimate of the value of output in each sector of the economy and in aggregate.

The three approaches never produce identically the same estimate, but they provide a good approximation to the value of aggregate income, expenditure and output.

E. Measuring Aggregate Income in Constant Dollars (Real)

To measure real income (output and expenditure), the expenditure approach is used. The final goods and services bought in each year are valued at the prices that prevailed in the base year.

F. Reading the National Income Accounts of the United States

The U.S. national income and product accounts are published by the Department of Commerce in the Survey of Current Business. The way in which the detailed items supplied in the published tables aggregate into the concepts employed in macroeconomics are set out in Table 3.2, and that table should be used as a reference guide.

Multiple Choice

Consider the following list of items and use it to answer the first two questions: (1) IBM shares, (2) government spending on espionage, (3) a computer, (4) a gas pipeline, (5) gas consumption, (6) expenditure on food, (7) wage payments, (8) the rate at which new cars are coming off an assembly line, (9) a car, (10) the price of a car.

1. a. Items (2), (5), (6), (7) and (8) are flows
   b. Items (2), (5), (6), (7), (8) and (9) are flows
   c. Items (2), (5), (6) and (8) are flows and all others are stocks
   d. Items (1), (2), (5), (6), (7), (8) and (10) are flows

2. a. Items (1), (3) and (4) are stocks and all others are flows
   b. Items (1), (3), (4) and (9) are stocks
   c. Items (1), (3), (9) and (10) are stocks and all others are flows
   d. Some items are stocks and some are flows

3. a. Gross domestic product at factor cost is equal to gross national expenditure at market prices less indirect taxes plus subsidies plus net property income paid to non-residents
   b. Gross domestic product at factor cost is equal to consumption plus investment plus government spending plus exports minus imports
   c. Gross national product at factor cost is equal to consumption plus investment plus government spending plus exports minus imports
   d. Gross national expenditure at market prices is always less than gross national product at factor cost

4. a. Real income in any given year is equal to expenditure in that year valued at the prices prevailing in the base year
   b. Real income is found by dividing nominal GNP by the Consumer Price Index
   c. The growth rate of real income includes the effects of inflation
   d. On the average the growth rate of nominal income and the growth rate of real income are the same

5. Consider the following list of items: (1) your purchase of a textbook, (2) IBM's purchase of microchips for use in computers, (3) American Airlines' purchase of jet fuel, (4) American Airlines' payment of wages to pilots, (5) American Airlines' purchase of a Boeing 747, (6) NASA's purchase of the Canada Arm for use in the Space Shuttle Columbia, (7) your purchase of a Big Mac, (8) the rental fee which you pay to a car rental company while on vacation, (9) the payment by a lawyer for the rental of his office, (10) your payment of your own phone bill. Items:

   a. (2), (3), (4), (5) and (6) are intermediate expenditures
   b. (1), (5), (6), (7), (8) and (10) are final expenditures
   c. (2), (3), (5) and (9) are intermediate expenditures
   d. (1), (5), (7), (8) and (10) are final expenditures

6. You are given the following information about an economy: Consumption is $600 million, investment is $100 million, indirect taxes are $100 million, government expenditure on goods and services is $150 million, exports are $200 million and imports are $180 million.

   a. GNP at factor cost is $870 million
   b. GNP at market prices is $770 million
   c. GNP at market prices is $870 million
   d. Net National Product is $500 million

7. You are given the same information as in Question 5 above and the additional information that income taxes are equal to $100 million.

   a. Savings are $50 million
   b. The government budget has a deficit of $50 million
   c. The balance of payments has a deficit of $20 million
   d. Savings are $70 million

8. You are given the following information: Wages are equal to $1000 million, consumption is $900 million, profits are $300 million, investment is $200 million, exports are $300 million, imports $200 million and income taxes are $200 million.

   a. GNP is $1200 million
   b. The government budget has a deficit of $100 million
   c. The government budget has a surplus of $100 million
   d. Savings are $250 million

9. You are given the following information: Gross national income is $1000 million, the government has a budget deficit of $100 million and there is a balance of payments deficit of $100 million and savings are $200 million.

   a. Consumption is $750 million
   b. Government spending is $150 million
   c. The sum of consumption and government spending is $800 million
   d. Investment is $200 million

True or False

1. You buy a car for $5,000 and you sell it two years later for $3,000. The difference between the two prices is a flow.

2. If the water in a bathtub is a stock then so is the rate at which water is flowing into and out of the tub for it is all the same water.

3. The relevant aggregate income concept for studying macroeconomic questions is gross national expenditure at market prices.

4. Net rather than gross measures of aggregate economic activity provide a more reliable guide to the value of current output in the economy.

5. In a simple closed economy with no government, savings and investment are equal to each other. The same is true in an open economy with a government.

6. If investment and savings are constant, a one million dollar rise in the government budget deficit must also be accompanied by a one million dollar rise in the balance of payments deficit.

7. If government spending and taxes are such that the government has a budget deficit, then savings must exceed investment, otherwise the country will experience a balance of payments deficit, or investment plus exports must exceed savings plus imports.

Fill in the Blanks

1. A macroeconomic flow is a ______ per unit of ______. In contrast, a stock is a value at a _______ in ___________. An example of a flow is ____________ or ____________. An example of a stock is the ______________________________ or the ______________________________.

2. To determine the value of gross ____________ product, it is necessary to add income paid to non-residents to gross ____________ product.

3. The difference between gross and net national product is ____________.

4. The difference between national expenditure at market prices and national income at factor cost is ____________________________.

Projects

1. Find, in your university library, the latest issue of Survey of Current Business. Using Tables 1.1, 1.5 and 1.7, construct Table 3.1 (page 47 of the textbook) for the most recent year available. Compare the most recent year with 1981 (Table 3.1, page 47 of textbook). Which of the items that add up to gross national product at market prices has grown most quickly and which the least quickly? By how much has gross national product at factor cost increased since 1981 expressed in terms of percent per annum changes? Can you figure out a way of separating that change into the change in real gross national product at factor cost and the change in prices?

2. Find, in your university library, an early copy of the Economic Report of the President, and from Table B-1 collect the following components of gross national product for the period of the Great Depression (1929-1937):

   a. consumption
   b. investment
   c. government expenditure
   d. exports
   e. imports
   f. gross national product

   For each series calculate the percentage change per annum, i.e., their annual growth rates. Plot these six time-series of the growth rates (1930-1937) all on the one graph. Use a different color for each series. Compare and contrast the paths of each of the components with that of gross national product. Which component has the most pronounced up-and-down swings in its annual growth rate?

Answers

Multiple Choice: 1 a 2 b 3 c 4 a 5 d 6 c 7 b 8 c 9 d
True or False: 1 T 2 F 3 F 4 F 5 F 6 T 7 T
Fill in the Blanks:
1. flow, time, point, time, income, expenditure, cash in my pocket on some particular day, volume of gas in the tank of my car at some point in time
2. domestic, national
3. capital consumption
4. indirect taxes less subsidies

CHAPTER 4

AGGREGATE BALANCE SHEET ACCOUNTING

By the time you have completed your study of this chapter you will:

(a) Understand the meaning of "asset", "liability", and "balance sheet".
(b) Know the definition of money and understand the nature of money.
(c) Know the main items in the balance sheets of households, firms, commercial banks, the central bank, government and the rest of the world.
(d) Know the main sources of information about aggregate balance sheets in the United States.

Chapter Summary

A. Asset Liability and Balance Sheet

An asset is what someone owns. A liability is what someone owes. There are two types of assets, financial and real. A financial asset is always someone else's financial liability. An individual's wealth equals total financial and real assets less total liabilities. A balance sheet is a statement of assets and liabilities.

B. Definition and Nature of Money

Money is anything that is generally acceptable as a medium of exchange. In the United States today, money is narrowly defined (M1) as the sum of notes and coins in circulation plus demand deposits. Money is defined more broadly (M2) as M1 plus (small-scale or short-term) savings deposits. A broader definition of money (M3) is M2 plus other (long-term or large-scale) bank deposits.

The monetary base is defined as the total liabilities of the Fed--notes outstanding plus banks' reserve deposits with the Fed--together with the stock of coin in circulation with the public.

C. Main Balance Sheet Items

Main balance sheet items are summarized in Tables 4.2 and 4.3 of the textbook (pp. 57, 60). The net value of financial assets in an economy is its net claims on the rest of the world. The change in net financial assets of the economy equals saving minus investment (S - I), plus taxes minus government expenditure (T - G), plus imports minus exports (IM - EX), which is always zero.

The aggregate of net claims on the rest of the world, nonhuman wealth, monetary base, and human wealth is the wealth of the economy.

A major part of the macroeconomic analysis that we shall be doing centers on the relationships between stocks and flows. In particular, it centers on the connection between the stock of money and the flows of expenditure. The theory of aggregate demand that we shall be developing shortly builds on the concepts that have been defined and on the accounting frameworks that are dealt with in this and in the previous chapter.

D. Measuring Aggregate Balance Sheets

The main coordinator of information about aggregate balance sheets in the United States is the Fed. It collects and publishes information about its own balance sheet, about those of the commercial banks, and about those of other financial institutions. It also collects information on and publishes the Flow of Funds Accounts. These accounts give information about changes in stocks rather than stocks themselves and do not include information about valuation changes.

The key stock variables needed for macroeconomic analysis are those concerning the monetary base and various definitions of the aggregate stock of money, all of which are collected frequently and reported in the Federal Reserve Bulletin.

Multiple Choice

1. a. Financial assets and liabilities always sum to zero for each individual sector of the economy
   b. An individual's wealth is equal to that individual's net financial assets plus real assets
   c. The larger an individual's financial assets, the wealthier is that individual
   d. Bank loans are assets to borrowers and liabilities to the bank

2. a. A Visa card is money
   b. A check is money
   c. The balance in a checking account is money
   d. A U.S. Savings Bond is money

3. a. M1 consists of all bank deposits
   b. M2 is bigger than M1
   c. The quantity of currency in circulation is not counted as part of M2
   d. Government demand deposits are part of M1

4. a. The monetary base consists of all the liabilities of the Fed plus currency in circulation
   b. The monetary base is equal to the assets of the Fed
   c. Currency holdings of the commercial banks are part of M1
   d. M1 includes all the assets in the monetary base

5. a. A government that has not issued bonds is wealthier than one that has
   b. Government securities are not part of the wealth of the economy because future tax liabilities exactly offset them
   c. The corporation that has undistributed profits is wealthier than one that does not
   d. The government can make people wealthier by borrowing more from them, thereby increasing their assets

6. a. The change in net financial assets of households and firms is equal to savings minus investment
   b. Since every financial asset has a corresponding financial liability, the change in financial assets is equal to the change in financial liabilities in each sector of the economy
   c. The government budget deficit is equal to the balance of payments deficit
   d. The change in the quantity of money is the same thing as the change in the net financial liabilities of banks

<u>True or False</u>

1. Since, when an individual borrows from the bank, he/she receives money that can be spent, a bank loan may be regarded as an asset to the borrower.

2. Unlike all other financial assets, money is no one's liability.

3. The monetary base is equal to the central bank's holdings of gold and foreign exchange.

4. The financial assets of one sector are the liabilities of other sectors.

5. Undistributed profits are reflected in the stock market value of the equity of a corporation and so are an asset to the households that own that corporation.

6. Future taxes will have to be raised to pay the interest on and/or redeem outstanding government debt. This means that government debt cannot be regarded as an asset by the people holding it.

7. There is no connection between the national balance sheet and the national income accounts. One measures stocks and the other flows.

8. The change in net financial assets of the foreign sector is equal to the value of imports less the value of exports.

9. The change in the net financial assets of the government sector is equal to the government's budget deficit.

10. The change in net financial assets of households and firms is equal to the value of savings minus investment.

<u>Fill in the Blanks</u>

1. The main financial assets of the household sector are:

   (a) ____________________ (b) ____________________

   (c) ____________________ (d) ____________________

   (e) ____________________ (f) ____________________

   (g) ____________________

2. The main financial liabilities of households are: __________________

3. The financial assets of firms are:

(a) ____________ (b) ____________

(c) ____________ (d) ____________

(e) ____________

4. The main financial liabilities of firms are:

(a) ____________ (b) ____________

(c) ____________

5. The main financial assets of banks are:

(a) ____________ (b) ____________

(c) ____________ (d) ____________

(e) ____________

6. The main financial liabilities of banks are:

(a) ____________ (b) ____________

7. The financial assets of the central bank (the Fed) are:

(a) ____________ (b) ____________

8. The financial liabilities of the Fed are:

(a) ____________ (b) ____________

9. The financial assets of the government sector are:

(a) ____________ (b) ____________

(c) ____________

10. The financial liabilities of the government sector are:

(a) ____________ (b) ____________

11. The change in net financial assets of households and firms in aggregate are equal to ____________ minus ____________.

12. The change in net financial assets of the government sector are equal to ____________ minus ____________.

13. The change in net financial assets of the rest of the world sector are ____________ minus ____________.

14. The sum of the change in net financial assets of households, firms, and the government sector is ________ minus ________ plus ________ minus ________, which is equal to ________ minus ________ .

Problem

The following is the list of financial assets and liabilities in an economy at the end of December 1983:

	$ billions
Notes and coins in circulation	10
Notes and coins held by commercial banks	1
Private checking accounts at commercial banks	18
Commercial bank deposits at the central bank	6
Savings accounts at the commercial banks	100
Commercial bank loans	105
Net foreign currency assets of the central bank	0.5
Net foreign liabilities of the commercial banks	2
Government securities held by commercial banks	10
Net government securities held by the central bank	15

Calculate:
(a) the monetary base
(b) total liabilities of the central bank
(c) liabilities of the government arising from the issue of coins
(d) the quantity of M1
(e) the quantity of M2
(f) the amount of private deposits other than checking and savings deposits at commercial banks

Answers

Multiple Choice: 1 b 2 c 3 b 4 a 5 b 6 a
True or False: 1 F 2 F 3 F 4 T 5 T 6 F 7 F 8 T 9 F 10 T
Fill in the Blanks:
1. currency, demand deposits at commercial banks, other bank deposits, government securities, equities, bonds, foreign securities
2. bank loans
3. currency, demand deposits at commercial banks, other bank deposits, government securities, foreign securities
4. bank loans, equities, bonds
5. deposits with the Fed, currency, government securities, bank loans, foreign securities
6. demand deposits, other bank deposits
7. government securities, foreign exchange
8. bank deposits, currency
9. demand deposits, other bank deposits, foreign exchange
10. government securities, coins
11. savings, investment
12. taxes, government spending
13. imports, exports
14. savings, investment, taxes, government spending, exports, imports

Problem: (a) $17 billion (b) $15.5 billion (c) $1.5 billion (d) $28 billion (e) $128 billion (f) $6 billion

CHAPTER 5

MEASURING INFLATION AND UNEMPLOYMENT

When you have completed your study of this chapter you will:

(a) Know the definition of inflation.
(b) Understand the concept of a price index and its percentage rate of change.
(c) Know how inflation is measured in the United States.
(d) Know the definition of unemployment.
(e) Know how unemployment is measured in the United States.

Chapter Summary

A. Definition of Inflation

Inflation is defined as the percentage rate of change in a price index.

B. Price Index and its Percentage Rate of Change

A price index is calculated by valuing a specific basket of goods at the prices prevailing in a base period and at the prices prevailing in a subsequent period. The price index is the ratio of the values of these two baskets multiplied by 100. The rate of inflation is measured as the percentage rate of change of the index.

C. Measuring Inflation in the United States

There are three commonly used price indexes in the United States: the Consumer Price Index (CPI), the Personal Consumption Expenditure (PCE) deflator, and the Gross National Product (GNP) deflator. The CPI is based on a fixed basket of goods and services typical of the consumption patterns of urban households. The PCE and GNP deflators are calculated on the basis of a current basket of goods and services, with the PCE deflator covering all consumption expenditures and the GNP deflator covering all consumption plus investment purchases and net exports.

D. Definition of Unemployment

Unemployment is defined as the number of people able and willing to work and available for work but not having work.

E. Measuring Unemployment in the United States

Unemployment is measured in the United States by the Current Population Survey, conducted each month. The survey records as unemployed all those who did not work during the survey week, but who made specific efforts to find a job within the 4 previous weeks, and who were available for work during the survey week. It also includes as unemployed those who were waiting to be called back to a job from which they had been laid off, as well as those waiting to report to a new job within 30 days.

Multiple Choice

1. Inflation is a situation:

   a. of rising food prices
   b. in which food prices are rising faster than clothing prices are falling
   c. in which there is a once-and-for-all overnight rise in the price level
   d. in which there is an ongoing rise in the general level of prices

2. A price index:

   a. is an alphabetical list of all goods and their prices
   b. is a weighted average of prices
   c. is a weighted average of prices prevailing at one time expressed as a percentage of those prevailing at another time
   d. measures inflation

3. The Consumer Price Index:

   a. measures the average cost of living of all Americans
   b. measures the cost of living of urban Americans
   c. is an index of the prices of thousands of goods
   d. is adjusted each month so that the weights are up-to-date

4. a. The GNP deflator gives a very different picture of inflation from the Consumer Price Index
   b. The weights used to calculate the GNP deflator are current
   c. The Consumer Price Index is the only true measure of inflation
   d. Inflation is measured by the absolute change in either the GNP deflator or the Consumer Price Index

5. a. A person is unemployed when that person is able and willing to work and is available for work but does not have work
   b. Anyone who is not working is unemployed
   c. A person is said to be unemployed only if the unemployment is "involuntary"
   d. Most of the unemployed are under the age of 17 and over the age of 65

6. a. No one has any idea how many people are unemployed in the United States
   b. The Department of Labor makes no systematic attempt to discover the wages at which unemployed persons would be willing to work
   c. The Department of Labor undertakes a massive monthly survey in order to assess the scale of unemployment in the United States
   d. To be counted as unemployed by the Department of Labor, a person must be lucky enough to be included in the sample of households surveyed

7. a. A person who has a new job to start within 30 days is not counted as being unemployed
   b. A person who has been laid off but is waiting to be called back to work is not counted as being unemployed even if the person is available for work
   c. No one who has not actively looked for work within the last 4 weeks is counted as being unemployed
   d. A person who is without work, has actually looked for work in the last 4 weeks, and is available for work will be counted as being unemployed

True or False

1. The CPI at date t measures the average price at date t of all goods consumed by U.S. households in some base year.

2. The basket of goods used in constructing the GNP deflator is the same as that used in constructing the CPI except that it includes some additional goods all of which are capital goods.

3. Inflation is measured by the rate of change of a price index. There are as many different measures of inflation as there are price indexes.

4. If a price index is 100 in 1980 and 120 in 1981, then the rate of inflation in 1981 was 20%.

5. If the CPI was 130 in 1982 and 125 in 1983, households on the average experienced 4% deflation in 1983.

The following would be counted as unemployed in the United States:

6. A steelworker laid off for 1 month who spends his time painting his house.

7. A person who has been permanently laid off from one job and who has been out of work for 6 months but has a new job to start next week.

8. A man who has quit one job to search for a better paying job.

9. A university graduate who can't find a job but is eager to work and who is still looking for his/her first job.

10. A worker laid off for 6 weeks who takes a job as a lift attendant at a ski resort in Colorado.

Fill in the Blanks

1. The rate of inflation is measured as the _______________ rate of change of _______________.

2. In the United States there are three commonly used price indexes:

   (i) _______________ (ii) _______________

   (iii) _______________

3. The ________________ and ________________ are implicit because ____.

4. In the base period the value of an index is _____.

5. If the value of the price index rises over time there has been ______________; if the value falls over time there has been ______________.

6. Unemployment is defined as the number of people: (i) ______________, (ii) ______________, but (iii) ________________.

7. The unemployment rate is ____.

8. Unemployment in the United States is estimated by a survey called ________________________________.

9. The survey in Question 8 interviews ______________ households each month.

10. The survey in Question 8 does not check whether the person interviewed was willing to work at ______________________.

Problems

1. An economy produces only three goods: oranges, cloth and concrete. In Year 0 (the base year) oranges sold for $1 a box, cloth for $10 a square yard and concrete for $100 a ton. In that year 1 million boxes of oranges were produced, 2 million square yards of cloth and 0.5 million tons of concrete. In the next year (Year 1) oranges sold for $1.25 per box, cloth $8 a square yard and concrete $120 a ton. Output in that year was 1.5 million boxes of oranges, 2 million square yards of cloth and 0.75 million tons of concrete. Consumers in this economy only buy oranges and cloth. Concrete is used for investment purposes and for purchases by the government. In Year 0 the representative consumer spent $300 per month, $100 on oranges and $200 on cloth. In Year 1 the representative consumer spent $365 a month, $125 on oranges and $240 on cloth.

   Calculate for Year 1:

   (i) Gross National Product in current prices
   (ii) Gross National Product in constant prices (base year prices)
   (iii) The GNP deflator
   (iv) The rate of inflation as measured by the GNP deflator
   (v) The Consumer Price Index
   (vi) The rate of inflation as measured by the Consumer Price Index

2. The Department of Labor runs a survey and interviews 50,000 people. It discovers that: 800 of these people had made no active effort to find work in the past 4 weeks though were in fact available for work and were waiting to be called back to a job from which they had been laid off; 967 of the people interviewed were discovered to be sick; 7,700 were retired; 3,800 were full-time housewives (or househusbands); 2,000 were without work and had been actively seeking work within the last 4 weeks and were available for work; 1,000 were taking a vacation; 533 were out of work but were available for work and had a new job that would start in less than 4 weeks; 3,200 of the people were students. The above categories sum to 20,000 people. Of these, 4,000 were receiving unemployment insurance benefits from the government; and 30,000 of the people surveyed had full-time jobs.

   Calculate the unemployment rate published by the Department of Labor on the basis of this survey.

Project

In the library of your university, find the latest copy of the Economic Report of the President. Using Table B-33 collect the unemployment rates for the following over the period 1950 to 1983:

(a) total male
(b) 16-19 year old male
(c) 20 years and over male
(d) total female
(e) 16-19 year old female
(f) 16-19 years both sexes
(g) white
(i) black and other

Draw 4 time-series graphs using the data collected in the following way. Firstly, draw a time-series graph that plots the series (a), (b) and (c). For the second time-series graph plot the series (d), (e) and (f). For the third time-series graph plot the time series (b), (e) and (f). For the fourth time-series graph plot the series (h) and (i). Describe each of these 4 graphs and then compare and contrast the time series within each of the graphs.

Answers

Multiple Choice: 1 d 2 c 3 b 4 b 5 a 6 b 7 d
True or False: 1 F 2 F 3 T 4 T 5 F 6 T 7 T 8 T 9 T 10 F
Fill in the Blanks:
1. percentage, price index
2. CPI, PCE deflator, GNP deflator
3. PCE deflator, GNP deflator, they are arrived at by two different evaluations
4. 100
5. inflation, deflation
6. able and willing to work, available for work, having no work
7. the number of people unemployed divided by the sum of the number of people employed and unemployed, converted to a percentage
8. Current Population Survey
9. 50,000
10. any current wage rate

Problems:
1. (i) $293.5m; (ii) $220m; (iii) 133.41; (iv) 33.41%; (v) 95; (vi) -5%
2. 7.79%

CHAPTER 6

THE BUSINESS CYCLE

When you have completed your study of this chapter you will:

(a) Know the definition of the business cycle.
(b) Understand the concept of autocorrelation.
(c) Understand the concept of co-movement.
(d) Know the properties of the business cycle.
(e) Know the features of the U.S. business cycle.

Chapter Summary

A. Definition of the Business Cycle

Business cycles are recurrent but non-periodic fluctuations in aggregate economic activity as measured by fluctuations in real GNP about its trend.

B. Autocorrelation

Autocorrelation is a technical term which means that the value of some variable is related to itself at some earlier date (or dates). An autocorrelated variable is described by a difference equation that is stochastically or randomly disturbed.

C. Co-movement

The term co-movement is used in the description of one variable in relation to another. Co-movements may be procyclical, in which case the two variables move up and down together; or countercyclical, in which case the two variables move in the opposite directions to each other. The cycle in one variable may lead or lag the cycle in another. The cycle in one variable may display a greater or smaller amplitude than the cycle in the other. Co-movement may display high conformity, in which case, the two series move in a similar manner; or low conformity, in which case, they do not move in close sympathy with each other.

D. Properties of the Business Cycle

Movements in real GNP about trend are well described by a first-order difference equation that is stochastically disturbed. In general, employment, prices, and interest rates are procyclical, and unemployment is countercyclical.

E. The U.S. Business Cycle

The general features of the business cycle set out above apply to the U.S. case, with the important observation that movements in inflation, although generally procyclical, are not universally so. There are important co-movements of inflation and unemployment that do not fit a simple pattern.

Multiple Choice

1. The business cycle is:

   a. a regular and predictable cycle in the level of aggregate economic activity
   b. completely random
   c. represented by movements in real GNP about its trend that are autocorrelated
   d. characterized by any up-and-down movement in any aggregate economic variable

2. a. A first-order difference equation cannot describe a cycle of any kind
   b. Cycles can only be described by sine waves like those used in physics
   c. Economic cycles are too irregular to be represented by any simple equation
   d. The fluctuations in real GNP around trend may be described by a first-order difference equation that is stochastically disturbed

3. The co-movements between two variables are procyclical:

   a. if they move up and down together
   b. if, when one moves up, the other moves down
   c. if there is no relationship at all between them
   d. when sometimes they move up and down together and at other times they move in opposite directions

4. a. Unemployment and real GNP are countercyclical
   b. Unemployment and inflation always move in opposite directions
   c. Interest rates and inflation are not related to each other in any systematic way
   d. Unemployment and inflation were strongly related to each other in the inter-war years, but have not been so strongly related since World War II

5. a. The business cycle usually has countercyclical interest rates
   b. A characteristic of the business cycle is that the deviation of output from trend of durable goods fluctuates with bigger amplitude than that of nondurable goods
   c. It is a feature of the business cycle that as employment in the agricultural sector falls, so in the manufacturing sector it rises
   d. A feature of the business cycle is that price movements are completely independent of movements in output

6. a. In the absence of new shocks, 16% of last year's deviation of real GNP from trend will, on the average, be eliminated in the current year in the United States
   b. Deviations of real GNP from trend in the United States cannot be described by any simple equation
   c. The U.S. business cycle is represented by a 2.6% trend growth rate in real GNP prior to 1946 and a 3.7% trend growth rate after 1946
   d. In the United States, every year is different--there is no cycle in output

True or False

1. The business cycle is a type of fluctuation in "aggregate economic activity". Unfortunately, however, the concept of "aggregate economic activity" is so vague as to make it impossible to provide an operational definition of the business cycle.

2. Autocorrelation is the correlation between one variable and another.

3. Autocorrelation shows that one variable causes another.

4. Autocorrelation is a useful descriptive device. It describes one variable as being correlated with its own earlier value (or values).

5. Unemployment has trended upwards so massively since the war that it cannot be regarded as having any relationship with the business cycle.

6. When interest rates drop, people like to borrow more and therefore spend more. This means that interest rates will be countercyclical.

7. The equation $(y_t - y_t^*) = .84(y_{t-1} - y_{t-1}^*) + e_t$ means that income always gradually converges towards y_t^* eliminating 84% of the previous year's deviation from y_t^*, every year. Such an equation is incompatible with the facts of the business cycle.

8. The equation $(y_t - y_t^*) = .84(y_{t-1} - y_{t-1}^*) + e_t$ is a complete <u>explanation</u> of the business cycle. No further or deeper explanation is needed.

9. The cause of the business cycle can be found by identifying the variable that fluctuates with the greatest amplitude.

10. Although inflation and unemployment are not perfectly correlated there is a strong tendency for inflation to be high when unemployment is low. It is, therefore, necessary to choose whether to have stable prices at the price of high unemployment, or low unemployment at the price of rapid inflation. The co-movements between inflation and unemployment provide no alternative to this.

Fill in the Blanks

1. The business cycle has four phases. They are: ______________, ______________, ______________, ______________.

2. If the value of a variable (such as deviations of real GNP from trend) is related in a systematic way to its own earlier value or values, then the variable is said to be ______________.

3. If two variables display cycles very similar to each other, each rising and falling together, they are said to possess ______________ ______________.

4. If two variables cycle together, but one goes up and the other goes down they are said to display __________ __________.

5. The central feature of the business cycle is that the deviations of __________ from trend can be well described by a __________ __________ __________ __________.

6. Over the business cycle inflation is generally (though not universally) __________.

7. Interest rates, over the business cycle, are __________.

8. Movements in real GNP about trend in the United States are well-described by a _____ order, _______________ disturbed difference equation.

Answers

Multiple Choice: 1 c 2 d 3 a 4 a 5 b 6 a
True or False: 1 F 2 F 3 F 4 T 5 F 6 F 7 F 8 F 9 F 10 F
Fill in the Blanks:
1. peak, trough, expansion, contraction
2. autocorrelated
3. procyclical co-movement
4. countercyclical co-movement
5. real GNP, first-order stochastic difference equation
6. procyclical
7. procyclical
8. first, stochastically

CHAPTER 7

INTRODUCTION TO THE BASIC MODEL

This brief chapter introduces the next part of the book. Before beginning to study this part, you should be sure that you are thoroughly familiar with:

(i) The questions that macroeconomics seeks to answer.
(ii) The main facts about the evolution of the key macroeconomic variables in the United States since 1900.
(iii) The way in which the macroeconomic variables are measured--aggregate income accounting, aggregate balance sheet accounting, the measurement of price indexes and inflation, and the measurement of unemployment.
(iv) How it is possible to characterize the ups and downs of activity and the co-movements among the variables as the business cycle.

You are now about to embark upon the more exciting, challenging and difficult problem of <u>explaining</u> macroeconomic phenomena--the study of macroeconomic theory.

When you have completed your study of this chapter you will:

(a) Know the reasons why you are going to study the basic model; and
(b) know the main weaknesses of that model. (You will only become convinced that they are weaknesses when you get to Chapter 13. It is worth knowing, however, in advance, what those weaknesses are so that you can maintain a critical eye as you work through the model.)

<u>Chapter Summary</u>

A. <u>Why Study the Basic Model?</u>

You are studying the basic model for three reasons:

1. Its ingredients are present in more complex and satisfactory models.
2. It shows why unemployment exists and some of the reasons why its rate varies.
3. It enables one to distinguish between inflation and a once-and-for-all rise in the price level, and to understand the causes of inflation.

B. <u>Weaknesses of the Basic Model</u>

The basic model is unable to explain the business cycle and severe and persistent depression.

CHAPTER 8

AGGREGATE SUPPLY AND THE LABOR MARKET

When you have completed your study of this chapter you will:

(a) Understand the concept of the short-run aggregate production function.
(b) Understand the working of a competitive aggregate labor market
(c) Understand the concept of the aggregate supply curve.

Chapter Summary

A. Short-Run Aggregate Production Function

The short-run aggregate production function shows how the maximum amount of output will vary as the number of workers employed varies while holding constant the stock of capital, the state of technology, and the skills of labor. Its properties are the same as the short-run production function of an individual firm in that it displays diminishing marginal productivity.

B. Competitive Aggregate Labor Market

A competitive aggregate labor market will determine an equilibrium real wage and level of employment where the downward sloping demand curve (derived from the marginal product curve) cuts an upward sloping labor supply curve (derived from utility maximizing decisions of households).

C. Aggregate Supply Curve

The aggregate supply curve shows how output varies as the price level varies when firms are maximizing profits, households are maximizing utility, and the labor market is in equilibrium. In the basic model developed in this chapter, aggregate supply is perfectly inelastic with respect to the price level.

Multiple Choice

1. The short-run production function tells us:

   a. the maximum output that can be produced in the economy
   b. how the maximum output that can be produced in the economy will vary as the inputs of all factors of production are varied
   c. how the maximum output that can be produced varies as the amount of labor employed varies
   d. how the maximum amount of output that can be produced will vary as the skills of labor are varied

2. The position of the short-run production function depends on:

   a. the number of people employed
   b. the wage paid
   c. the quantity of fixed inputs
   d. the type of returns to scale

3. The short-run production function has:

   a. constant returns to scale--if the inputs of all factors of production are doubled, so output will be doubled
   b. increasing returns to scale--if the inputs of all factors of production are doubled, output will more than double
   c. decreasing returns to scale--if the inputs of all factors of production are doubled, output will less than double
   d. diminishing marginal productivity--if all inputs except labor are held constant, then a rise in the input of labor will raise output but by diminishing incremental amounts

4. In a competitive economy:

   a. firms will demand labor so long as the average cost of labor does not exceed the average output per head
   b. once a firm has hired a certain quantity of labor, it will keep that labor on no matter what happens to the real wage
   c. firms will pay whatever is necessary to attract the best workers
   d. firms will hire labor up to the point at which the marginal product of that labor is equal to the real wage

5. A firm that has a monopoly in the market for its output:

   a. will hire more labor than the firm would in a competitive industry because a monopolist can afford to pay higher wages
   b. demands less labor than it would in a competitive industry
   c. has a larger elasticity of demand for its output and a smaller demand for labor than a firm in a competitive industry
   d. is not constrained by the theory of the demand for labor

6. The supply of labor:

   a. will always slope upwards even if households have a choice over their hours of work
   b. will slope up if households have to make an all-or-nothing choice--when they have to choose whether to work or not work and for a fixed number of hours
   c. curve slopes downwards as people will work harder at lower wages because they have to earn enough to eat
   d. is socially determined and is independent of the level of wages

7. Equilibrium in the labor market:

   a. occurs when firms have filled all the jobs they have available
   b. occurs even if firms cannot fill all the jobs they have available, so long as no one is unemployed
   c. occurs when the supply of labor equals the demand for labor
   d. can occur at any wage rate because workers have to have jobs regardless of how much they are paid

8. Aggregate supply:

   a. is the maximum level of output that the economy can produce
   b. rises as the real wage rate rises
   c. falls as the real wage rate rises
   d. is the output produced when the labor market is in equilibrium

9. If the price level rises:

   a. then aggregate supply also rises
   b. aggregate supply falls
   c. aggregate supply is independent of the price level--at a given price level any amount could be supplied
   d. aggregate supply is unchanged as it is independent of the price level

10. a. The level of employment is independent of the price level
    b. If the price level rises, then the real wage falls
    c. Any fall in the real wage will create more jobs as firms move down the demand for labor curve
    d. An improvement in technology which raises labor's productivity shifts the supply of labor curve to the left as not as many people are now required to produce the same output

<u>True or False</u>

In a competitive economy, the aggregate production function is

$$y = 6n$$

The supply of labor is

$$n^s = 1000(W/P)$$

The marginal product of labor is 6 and the price of one unit of output is \$6.00.

1. The equilibrium real wage is 36.

2. The equilibrium real wage is 6.

3. The equilibrium level of employment is 6000.

4. The equilibrium level of output is 3600.

5. The equilibrium money wage rate is \$36.

6. The level of employment if the price level rises to \$7.00 is 6000.

7. The level of output if the price level falls to \$5.00 is 36,000.

8. The equation to the AS curve is $y = 36{,}000$.

9. If the price level rises 10% the real wage remains constant and the money wage rises 10%.

10. Changes in the price level do not affect changes in the real variables such as output and employment.

Fill in the Blanks

1. The short-run aggregate production function shows how the ___________ amount of output will vary as the number of workers employed varies holding constant the (i) ___________, the (ii) ___________, and (iii) ___________.

2. The supply of labor curve is ___________ sloping. It shows the quantity of labor that is willingly supplied as the ___________ rises so that households maximize their ___________.

3. The demand for labor curve is ___________ sloping. This shows that firms would only be willing to hire more labor at a ___________ real wage. Along the demand for labor curve firms are maximizing ___________.

4. In a competitive labor market the real wage is ___________, and the level of employment is ___________, as the price level varies.

5. The aggregate supply curve is ___________ . This shows that as the price level varies output ___________________________ .

Problems

1. An economy consists of a thousand firms. Each firm has a short-run production function given by the following table:

no. of men	1	2	3	4	5	6	7	8	9	10
output	12	40	66	90	112	132	150	166	180	192

As the wage rate increases, more men will be willing to supply their labor. Specifically, the following is the relationship between the wage rate and the number of men willing to work:

wage rate ($)	90	100	110	120	130	140	150	160	180	200
no. of men	1000	2000	3000	4000	5000	6000	7000	8000	9000	10,000

The price level is $10.

a. Draw the short-run production function for an individual firm
b. Calculate the marginal product of labor at each level of employment
c. Draw the marginal product of labor curve
d. Plot the aggregate demand for labor curve
e. Plot the aggregate supply of labor curve

Calculate:

f. the equilibrium money wage rate
g. the equilibrium real wage rate

h. the equilibrium level of employment
i. the equilibrium level of output
j. the equilibrium level of the total wage bill and total profits of the firms

2. Suppose that in the economy described in Question 1 the price level doubles to become $20. State what happens to:

   a. the production function
   b. the marginal product of labor
   c. the supply curve of labor--the money wage needed to induce a given labor supply
   d. the equilibrium real wage rate
   e. the equilibrium employment level
   f. the equilibrium level of output
   g. the equilibrium money wage rate

3. (This is a harder question.)
   Suppose that the entire industry described in Question 1 became monopolized and that the monopolist faced an elasticity of demand equal to -2. State what happens to:

   a. the demand for labor curve--the money wage needed to induce a given demand for labor

   Calculate:

   b. the equilibrium level of employment
   c. the equilibrium real wage
   d. the equilibrium level of output
   e. the equilibrium money wage
   f. the equilibrium total wage bill
   g. the equilibrium level of profits
   h. the share of national income earned in profits
   i. the share of national income earned in wages

Project

In your university library find an early copy of the Economic Report of the President (Washington, D.C.: U.S. Government Printing Office), and collect the following data for the period of the Great Depression (1929 to 1937):

(a) GNP in constant dollars (i.e. output)
(b) average gross hourly earnings, total private nonagricultural (i.e. the money wage)
(c) average weekly hours, total private nonagricultural (i.e. the number of hours employed)
(d) the labor force
(e) the CPI

and calculate:

(f) the real wage by dividing (b) by (e).

On some graph paper, create three graphs by plotting the point for each year on the production function, the demand for labor curve and the supply of labor curve.

Can you draw a smooth curve of the appropriate shape through the points for successive years to generate one production function, one demand for labor curve and one supply of labor curve? If you cannot do so, try to show how each of these three curves must have shifted during the Great Depression. Can you think of a reason why each curve may have shifted?

Answers

Multiple Choice: 1 c 2 c 3 d 4 d 5 b 6 b 7 c 8 d 9 d 10 a
True or False: 1 F 2 T 3 T 4 F 5 F 6 T 7 T 8 T 9 T 10 T
Fill in the Blanks:
1. maximum, stock of capital, state of technology, labor skills
2. upward, real wage, utility
3. downward, lower, profits
4. constant, constant
5. vertical, remains constant

Problems:
1. (f) \$160 (g) 16 (h) 8,000 (i) 166,000 (j) \$1,280,000, \$380,000
2. (a), (b), (d), (e) and (f) remain the same, (c) shifts up so that the money wage doubles, (g) doubles
3. (a) shifts down so that the money wage halves (b) 4,000 (c) 12 (d) 90,000 (e) \$120 (f) \$480,000 (g) \$420,000 (h) 46.7% (i) 53.3%

CHAPTER 9

AGGREGATE DEMAND IN THE MONEY MARKET

When you have completed your study of this chapter you will:

(a) Understand the concept of aggregate demand.
(b) Understand the monetary theory of aggregate demand.

Chapter Summary

A. Aggregate Demand

Aggregate demand is the demand for all final goods and services--the demand for output. The aggregate demand curve is the relationship between the price level and the demand for output.

B. The Monetary Theory of Aggregate Demand

The monetary theory of aggregate demand states that the level of aggregate demand will fall as the price level rises. It also states that aggregate demand will rise as the money supply rises. These propositions are derived from the assumption that the amount of money which people want to hold is proportional to the price level, rises as real income rises, and falls as the inflation rate rises. Equilibrating forces ensure that, in the normal course of events, the supply of money equals the demand for money and that the amount of goods and services demanded is proportional to the supply of real money balances.

Multiple Choice

1. Aggregate demand is:

   a. the total demand in the economy for all goods and services produced there plus the demand for imports
   b. the total demand for all goods and services produced in the economy
   c. the total demand for all final goods and services produced in the economy
   d. the sum of the demands for goods and services by households and the government

2. a. The demand for money is a stock
   b. Actual money holdings is a flow
   c. The demand for money is always infinite as it is the amount of money which people would like to have to spend and that is always an infinite amount
   d. If a person is paid monthly then his demand for money decreases from the beginning of the month to the end of it

3. The demand for money:

a. equals the actual holdings of money
b. is the average holding of money
c. varies over the year
d. is the average holding of money and this varies over the year

4. a. If money income rises the propensity to hold money rises
b. If interest rates rise the propensity to hold money also rises
c. The propensity to hold money does not depend upon the inflation rate
d. The higher is the inflation rate, the lower is the propensity to hold money

5. A person will economize on his holdings of money balances if:

a. the interest rate rises
b. the inflation rate falls
c. his income rises
d. there is a once-and-for-all rise in the price level

6. A person economizes on his holdings of money balances if:

a. he transfers some of the cash in his pockets into his savings account
b. he switches funds from his savings account into his checking account
c. he increases his holdings of bonds
d. he buys a house

7. The demand for money:

a. is independent of the size of real income
b. rises as inflation rises
c. falls as the nominal interest rate rises
d. rises as the nominal interest rate rises

8. If the supply of money exceeds the demand for it, then:

a. the price level will rise
b. output will rise
c. nominal income will rise
d. The demand for money automatically increases so that it always equals the supply of money, and is totally independent of the level of output or income as the supply of money is, by definition, the amount of money that people hold

9. Aggregate demand is inversely proportional to:

a. the money supply
b. the marginal propensity to hold money
c. the price level
d. the demand for money

True or False

1. As the inflation rate rises, people try to stock up on goods and so they demand more money in order to be able to buy these goods.

2. As the inflation rate rises, the demand for money rises and this leads to a rise in the money supply.

3. The demand for real money balances rises as the inflation rate rises.

4. The demand for real money balances is inversely related to the rate of inflation.

5. The demand for money is just another name for the propensity to hold money.

6. A man earns $2,000 each month and spends his earnings evenly throughout the month. His demand for money is $1,000 and his propensity to hold money is .5.

7. A man earns $2,000 each month. As soon as he receives his pay he deposits $1,000 in his savings account. His demand for money is $500 and his propensity to hold money is 1/24.

8. If the supply of money rises, aggregate demand for goods and services rises.

9. If the nominal rate of interest rises, this leads to a rise in aggregate demand.

10. As long as the rate of inflation is constant, the nominal rate of interest and the real rate of interest are the same.

Fill in the Blanks

1. Aggregate demand is the demand for ____ _________ goods and services

2. Aggregate demand ___________ as the price level rises, and ___________ as the money supply rises.

3. The demand for real balances ___________ as real income rises, and ___________ as the inflation rate rises.

4. Along the aggregate demand curve the ___________ market is in equilibrium.

5. As the supply of real money balances rises so the aggregate demand curve shifts to the ___________ .

Problem

On the 1st of June a student starts work at a summer camp. The student receives and spends no money while working at the camp and is fed and housed by the organizers of the camp. On August 31st, the student is paid $5,600 for the work during the summer. Immediately when the pay check is received the student pays his/her tuition fees of $1,000, a month's rent of $150, and puts $4,200 in a savings account that pays a high rate of interest but which can only be withdrawn by giving one month's notice. During the month of September the student spends the balance of his/her income (that has not already been spent or placed in the savings account) at an even rate. Each month thereafter the student withdraws $400 from his/her savings account on the first day of the month and immediately pays that month's rent of $150. The remaining amount withdrawn is spent at an even rate through the month. On January 1st the student withdraws $1,000 extra which is used immediately to pay the second semester's tuition fees. On May 31st the student withdraws his/her interest on the savings deposit and spends it immediately. The student then departs for another long summer of hard work at the camp, at which point the above story repeats.

Calculate the student's:

(a) average money holding
(b) propensity to hold money

Answers

Multiple Choice: 1 c 2 a 3 b 4 d 5 a 6 a 7 c 8 c 9 b
True or False: 1 F 2 F 3 T 4 T 5 F 6 F 7 T 8 T 9 T 10 F
Fill in the Blanks:
1. all final
2. falls, rises
3. rises, falls
4. money
5. right
Problem: (a) 93.75 (b) 0.017

CHAPTER 10

EQUILIBRIUM IN THE BASIC MODEL

This chapter brings together the labor market and the determination of aggregate supply of goods and services which was studied in Chapter 8, and the money market and the determination of aggregate demand which was studied in Chapter 9. When you have completed your study of this chapter you will: Understand how the equality of aggregate supply and of aggregate demand for goods and labor determines the level of output, employment, the real wage, the money wage and the price level.

Chapter Summary

When the amount of money which people wish to hold is equal to the money supply and when producers are unable to increase their profits by changing their output and employment, then the economy is in equilibrium. It is the essence of the basic model that the equilibrating forces are sufficiently strong for the economy normally to be observed only at equilibrium.

Multiple Choice

1. Aggregate demand is always equal to aggregate supply because:

   a. aggregate demand adjusts
   b. aggregate supply always adjusts
   c. the Fed always changes the money supply to make it so
   d. price level adjusts to make it so

2. If the economy is:

   a. on the AS curve, then the money market is in equilibrium
   b. on the AD curve, then firms are maximizing their profits
   c. at the intersection of the AD and AS curves, households are maximizing utility but firms are not maximizing profits
   d. on the AS curve, then both households are maximizing utility and firms are maximizing profits

3. At any point:

   a. to the right of the aggregate demand curve there is excess supply in the money market
   b. to the left of the aggregate demand curve there is excess supply in the money market
   c. to the right of the AS curve the price level is too high
   d. above the AD curve the price level is too high

4. a. On the AS curve the labor market is in equilibrium
   b. Along the AD curve the inflation rate varies
   c. The AS curve shifts to the right if the money supply rises
   d. A rise in the price level lowers aggregate demand so the AD curve shifts to the left

5. As the level of aggregate demand rises:

a. the price level and the real wage both rise
b. the level of employment and the level of output both rise
c. the only thing that adjusts is the price level
d. the price level rises and so too does the money wage; all real variables remain constant

6. If aggregate demand does not equal aggregate supply, then:

a. firms always adjust the level of employment and output to make aggregate supply equal aggregate demand
b. households spend more so as to make aggregate demand equal aggregate supply
c. the Fed adjusts the money supply to make it so
d. the price level adjusts to make it so

7. a. A rise in the inflation rate will shift AD upwards and cause the price level to rise
b. A rise in the rate of inflation will cause the prices of goods to rise. This causes the profits of firms to be increased and so firms will hire more labor. Thus the rise in inflation is associated with a fall in unemployment
c. If the Fed raises the money supply, then households will buy more goods and this will encourage firms to hire more people. Thus a rise in the money supply and a fall in unemployment always go together
d. If people decided to work harder, the real wage would rise because the supply of labor curve shifts to the left. This causes the level of employment and output to fall. So an increase in the productivity of labor is always associated with a rise in unemployment

8. If the income payment interval for all households is halved, then:

a. the demand for money rises
b. aggregate demand is unaffected
c. the price level falls
d. the money supply falls

9. If more firms are willing to accept checks, then:

a. the demand for money falls
b. the price level remains constant
c. the price level rises
d. aggregate demand rises

10. a. The money wage rises as the demand for final goods rises
b. The money wage falls as the level of employment falls
c. The money wage never falls as workers will not work at a money wage which is unfair
d. Shifts in aggregate supply never affect the money wage

11. In the basic model:

a. everyone in the economy has a job
b. everyone who wants to work finds a job
c. the labor market is always in equilibrium
d. there are no fluctuations in employment

True or False

1. The level of aggregate demand at full-employment output determines the price level.

2. At the equilibrium output and price level the money market, the goods market and the labor market are all in equilibrium.

3. A 10% rise in the money supply raises the price level but by less than 10%.

4. A rise in labor productivity raises the real wage, raises output and raises the price level.

5. A fall in the money supply lowers the price level, lowers the money wage and increases the number of people employed.

6. A once-and-for-all rise in the money supply does not raise the inflation rate.

7. A continuous rise in the money supply of 10% leads to 10% inflation.

8. The basic model always adjusts slowly towards the equilibrium. As the amount of money people hold is the money supply, the money market is always in equilibrium so that the path to the equilibrium is along the aggregate demand curve.

9. In the basic model everyone in the economy always has a job.

10. In the basic model there is never a cycle in output around its full-employment level.

Fill in the Blanks

1. A once-and-for-all drop in the money supply of 5% ____________ the price level by ______%.

2. A continuous decline in the money supply of 5% per annum leads to ____________ of 5%. Real wages remain constant so that money wages ____________ by 5%.

3. A once-and-for-all rise in the price level of 4% is ______ the same thing as an inflation rate of 4%. A once-and-for-all rise in the price level occurs at ____________, whereas inflation is an ____________ process.

4. Equilibrium in the labor market determines the level of ___________ which with the production function determines the full-employment level of ___________ . The money supply determines the level of aggregate ___________ . The price level is determined by the intersection of aggregate ___________ and aggregate ___________ .

Problems

1. Assume the following hypothetical economy:

   1. $y = 20n - 0.1n^2$
   2. $n^s = 5(W/P)$
   3. $n^d = 100 - 5(W/P)$
   4. $M^d = 0.2Py$
   5. $M = 150$

   where y is output, n is the number of people employed, n^s is the supply of labor, W is the money wage, P is the price level, M^d is the demand for money, M is the money supply.

   (a) What is the equation to the AS curve?
   (b) What is the equation to the AD curve?

   Calculate:

   (c) the equilibrium level of output
   (d) the equilibrium level of employment
   (e) the equilibrium real wage
   (f) the equilibrium price level
   (g) the equilibrium money wage

2. Assume the hypothetical economy in Question 1 above. If the money supply rose to 180, what now are the answers to (a) to (g) above?

Answers

Multiple Choice: 1 d 2 d 3 b 4 a 5 d 6 d 7 a 8 c 9 b 10a 11 c
True or False: 1 T 2 T 3 F 4 F 5 F 6 T 7 T 8 F 9 F 10 F
Fill in the Blanks:
1. lowers, 5
2. deflation, fall
3. not, an instant, ongoing
4. employment, aggregate output, demand, demand, supply

Problems:
1. (a) $y = 750$ (b) $y = 750/P$ (c) 750 (d) 50 (e) 10 (f) 1 (g) \$10
2. (a) $y = 750$ (b) $y = 900/P$ (c) 750 (d) 50 (e) 10 (f) 1.2 (g) \$12

CHAPTER 11

UNEMPLOYMENT

When you have finished your study of this chapter you will:

(a) Understand how minimum wage laws create unemployment.
(b) Understand how labor unions raise wages and create unemployment.
(c) Understand how unemployment insurance programs create unemployment.
(d) Understand how taxes affect unemployment.

Chapter Summary

A. Minimum Wage Laws and Unemployment

Minimum wage laws raise the economy average real wage above the competitive equilibrium level. With voluntary exchange this means that the number of people employed will be less than the competitive equilibrium quantity and the number of people who would like jobs will be greater than the competitive equilibrium quantity. There will, therefore, be a rise in the real wage, a fall in employment, a rise in the labor force, and a rise in unemployment.

B. Labor Unions and Unemployment

An economy-wide labor union has exactly the same types of effects as a government-enforced minimum wage law.

A labor union which does not control the whole economy, but which leaves some part of the economy competitive will have the effect of raising the real wage and lowering the employment in the union sector while the real wage will fall and employment will rise in the nonunion sector. In such a case no unemployment will be created. If, however, the labor union successfully lobbies for minimum wages, then unemployment will arise but because of the minimum wage, not because of the union wage-setting activity.

C. Unemployment Insurance Benefits and Unemployment

The introduction of an unemployment insurance program lowers the cost of job search and makes job search more attractive than both work and leisure at the margin. Therefore, it raises the labor force and cuts the supply of labor; the equilibrium real wage rises, employment falls, the labor force rises, and unemployment rises.

D. Taxes and Unemployment

If the level of taxes is increased, there will be a fall in the level of employment and a rise in labor's share of national income. The fall in employment will manifest itself as measured unemployment if the workers who withdraw from labor avail themselves of unemployment insurance benefits to which they have earned an entitlement.

Multiple Choice

1. Minimum wage laws:

   a. raise the level of employment
   b. raise the economy average wage
   c. lower unemployment
   d. raise output

2. Minimum wages:

   a. do not affect the equilibrium wage
   b. do not create unemployment
   c. raise the economy average real wage
   d. do not affect the number of people employed

3. An economy-wide union:

   a. protects consumers
   b. protects all its members
   c. raises unemployment
   d. raises employment

4. If only half the labor force is unionized:

   a. the economy is competitive
   b. the union redistributes income between the unionized and non-unionized sectors
   c. wages are the same as in the competitive economy
   d. everyone wants to work in the unionized sector

5. The introduction of an unemployment insurance program:

   a. raises the cost of job search
   b. does not change the cost of job search
   c. makes leisure more attractive
   d. makes job search more attractive than work

6. Introducing more attractive unemployment benefits:

   a. rotates the supply of job search to the right
   b. shifts the supply of job search upwards
   c. shifts the labor force curve upwards
   d. rotates the supply of labor curve to the right

7. Introducing more attractive unemployment insurance benefits:

   a. lowers the supply of labor and raises the labor force
   b. raises the supply of labor and lowers the labor force
   c. raises the supply of labor and raises the labor force
   d. lowers the supply of labor and lowers the labor force

8. Introducing a tax on labor income:

   a. lowers employment
   b. lowers the real wage
   c. lowers unemployment
   d. raises the after-tax wage

9. The introduction of an employment tax:

   a. reduces the supply of labor
   b. shifts the demand for labor curve to the right
   c. shifts the demand for labor curve to the left
   d. shifts both the demand for and the supply of labor curves to the left

True or False

1. A cut in the benefits of an unemployment insurance program reduces the value placed on leisure, lowers the value placed on job search, and encourages less people to work.

2. An improvement in unemployment insurance benefits raises the price level.

3. A rise in minimum wages raises the money supply.

4. A drop in minimum wages cuts employment and output.

5. As more people join a union, wages are pushed up and so the supply of labor curve shifts to the right.

6. As taxes on employment are increased, labor's share of national income rises, while the share accruing to the owners of capital decreases.

Fill in the Blanks

1. Minimum wage laws ____________ the economy average real wage ____________ the competitive equilibrium level. This leads to a ____________ in employment, a ____________ in the labor force and a ____________ in unemployment.

2. An economy-wide union __________________ unemployment or inflation.

3. An improvement in unemployment insurance benefits ____________ the cost of job search and makes job search ____________ attractive than work and ____________ attractive than leisure at the margin. This leads to a ____________ in the labor force, a ____________ in employment, a ____________ in the real wage and a ____________ in unemployment.

4. As the level of taxes is increased, the level of employment ___________, labor's share of national income ___________, and unemployment ___________.

Problems

1. Suppose the labor market in some economy is described in the following way: The demand for labor is

$$n^d = 10 - 0.5(W/P)$$

The supply of labor is

$$n^s = 0.5(W/P)$$

The supply of job search is

$$j^s = 0.1(W/P)$$

Calculate:

(a) the equilibrium real wage
(b) the equilibrium level of employment
(c) the equilibrium labor force
(d) the equilibrium level of unemployment
(e) the value placed on job search by the last (marginal) person in employment
(f) the value placed on job search by the last (marginal) member of the labor force

If the government introduces a minimum real wage of 12, calculate:

(g) the level of employment
(h) the supply of labor
(i) the labor force
(j) the additional unemployment created by the minimum wage

2. An economy has a labor supply schedule given by:

real wage	1	2	3	4	5	6	7	8	9	10
labor supply	10	20	30	40	50	60	70	80	90	100

It has a supply of job search schedule given by:

real wage	1	2	3	4	5	6	7	8	9	10
job search	1	2	5	10	20	25	30	35	40	50

The production function of each of 10 firms in this economy is:

employment	1	2	3	4	5	6	7	8	9	10
output	20	37	44	50	55	59	62	64	65	64

Calculate:

(a) the equilibrium real wage
(b) the equilibrium level of employment
(c) the equilibrium level of job search
(d) the equilibrium size of the labor force
(e) the value placed on job search by the marginal person hired
(f) the value placed on job search by the marginal person to join the labor force

Project

In your university library, find a recent copy of the Economic Report of the President (Washington, D.C.: Government Printing Office) and collect the following participation rates from 1955:

(a) all civilian workers
(b) white males
(c) white females
(d) black and other males
(e) black and other females
(f) white females, 20 years and over
(g) black and other females, 20 years and over

On some graph paper, plot these seven times series. Use a different color for each different time series. Describe each of the series. Compare and contrast each of them. Which series have increased faster than the series (a)? Can you think of a reason why this has happened?

Answers

Multiple Choice: 1 b 2 c 3 c 4 b 5 d 6 a 7 a 8 a 9 c
True or False: 1 F 2 T 3 F 4 F 5 F 6 T
Fill in the Blanks:
1. raise, above, fall, rise, rise
2. does not create
3. lowers, more, more, rise, fall, rise, rise
4. falls, rises, rises

Problems
1. (a) 10 (b) 5 (c) 6 (d) 1 (e) 12/3 (f) 2 (g) 4 (h) 6 (i) 7.2 (j) 2.2
2. (a) 5 (b) 50 (c) 20 (d) 70 (e) 1 (f) 2

CHAPTER 12

INFLATION

When you have completed your study of this chapter you will:

(a) Know the distinction between a once-and-for-all rise in the price level and inflation.
(b) Know the effects on the price level of the following labor market shocks: a rise in the legislated minimum wage, a labor union induced wage rise, a rise in unemployment insurance benefits and a rise in taxes.
(c) Understand how a continuing growth in the money supply leads to inflation.

Chapter Summary

A. Once-and-for-all Price Level Rises and Inflation

Inflation is an ongoing process of persistently rising prices. A once-and-for-all rise in the price level occurs when the price level moves from one steady-state level to another steady-state level.

B. The Price Level and Labor Market Shocks

A rise in the legislated minimum wage, a labor union induced wage rise, a rise in the scale of unemployment insurance benefits and a rise in taxes on labor all have the effect of raising the real wage and lowering the level of employment. A lower level of employment will generate a lower level of output, and therefore, aggregate supply will fall. A lower level of aggregate supply will induce a higher price level. The percentage rise in the price level will equal the percentage fall in output. Thus, these shocks will have the effect of generating a once-and-for-all rise in the price level.

C. Money Supply Growth and Inflation

A continuing growth in the money supply leads to inflation. The steady-state rate of inflation will equal the rate of growth of the money supply minus the rate of growth of output. A rise in the rate of growth of the money supply will cause the rate of inflation to "overshoot" its steady-state value and to approach the steady state from above.

Multiple Choice

1. Minimum wages lead to:

   a. a once-and-for-all rise in the price level
   b. a rise in the inflation rate
   c. a rise in aggregate supply
   d. a rise in aggregate demand

2. a. A cut in unemployment insurance benefits reduces inflation
   b. A rise in the minimum wage raises inflation
   c. An increase in union membership raises inflation
   d. A rise in unemployment insurance benefits leaves inflation unchanged

3. a. A once-and-for-all drop in the money supply reduces aggregate supply
   b. A once-and-for-all rise in the price level does not shift the aggregate demand curve
   c. Any change in the price level is a change in the inflation rate
   d. A rise in the money supply lowers unemployment

4. a. An inflation rate of 10% is created if the money supply growth rate rises by 10%
   b. An ongoing inflation rate of 10% means that money wages are falling continuously by 10%
   c. A money supply growth rate of 10% will cause the aggregate demand curve to be continuously shifting upwards by 10% and so leads to an inflation rate of 10%
   d. A 10% inflation rate leads to a drop in the propensity to hold money and so the aggregate demand curve shifts up but by less than 10%

5. a. Steady-state inflation is equal to the sum of the growth rate of output and the money supply growth rate
   b. The money supply growth rate overshoots the inflation rate as people try to save for the future
   c. Steady-state output growth rate is determined by the money supply growth rate and the inflation rate
   d. At a steady-state output growth rate of 3%, the difference between the steady-state levels of inflation and the money supply growth rate is -3%

6. a. When inflation rises people save more
   b. If the steady-state rate of money growth falls, inflation falls gradually to approach the new money supply growth rate
   c. If inflation falls this leads to a drop in the money supply which for some time is bigger than the drop in the inflation rate
   d. A drop in the steady-state money supply growth rate will lead to people economizing on their money holdings and so the drop in inflation exceeds that in the money supply growth for some time but not permanently

7. A rise in the steady-state rate of growth of the money supply from 5% to 10% when the steady-state rate of growth of output is constant:

   a. raises the inflation rate from 5% to 10%
   b. raises inflation by more than 5 percentage points for some time but not forever
   c. causes the inflation rate to cycle upwards to its new steady-state level
   d. raises the price level by 5 percentage points

8. a. If the money supply growth rate is 10%, inflation is 10% and the growth rate of real income is 3% the economy is in the steady-state
   b. If real income and the money supply are both growing at 5% then the inflation rate is also 5%
   c. If steady-state real income growth rate rose 1% and the money supply growth rate was constant, the new steady-state inflation rate falls by 1%
   d. If the steady-state money supply growth rate is 10%, inflation is 10%

True or False

1. A rise in the minimum wage raises the price level but does not change the inflation rate.

2. A labor market shock that lowers the level of aggregate supply will raise the price level by the same percentage as the fall in output.

3. A once-and-for-all rise in the money supply of 10% does not lead to inflation of 10% but leads to a once-and-for-all rise in the price level of 10%.

4. The steady-state rate of growth of output will be equal to the steady-state rate of growth of the money supply plus the steady-state rate of inflation.

5. An economy with 2% real income growth and 7% money supply growth is experiencing steady-state inflation of 5%. If the money supply growth rate rises to 12% and stays there, the rate of inflation will gradually rise to 10% and stay there.

Fill in the Blanks

1. Inflation is an ____________ process of persistently rising prices.

2. A rise in the legislated minimum wage or a rise in unemployment insurance benefits leads to a ____________ rise in the price level.

3. A rise in unemployment insurance benefits which produces a 4% rise in the price level also induces a _____% ________ in output.

4. A continuing growth in the money supply leads to ____________. A once-and-for-all rise in the money supply leads to a __________________ rise in the price level.

5. In the steady-state the rate of inflation equals the rate of growth of ____________ minus the rate of growth of ____________.

6. If in the steady-state the money supply growth rate is 12% per annum and if output is growing at 5% per annum, then the steady-state inflation rate is ______% per annum

7. When there is a fall in the steady-state rate of growth of the money supply, inflation ____________ and ____________ the new steady-state rate of growth of the money supply en route to its new ____________ level.

Problem:

Initially the economy is in the steady-state with a money supply growth rate of 10% per annum and inflation of 3% per annum. At time t_1 the money supply growth rate is increased to 13% per annum and held there forever.

Calculate:

(a) the steady-state growth rate of real income
(b) the new steady-state money supply growth rate
(c) the new steady-state inflation rate

and describe the path of each of the following from time t_1 onwards:

(d) the money supply growth rate
(e) the real income growth rate
(f) the inflation rate

Answers

Multiple Choice: 1 a 2 d 3 b 4 c 5 d 6 d 7 b 8 c
True or False: 1 T 2 T 3 T 4 F 5 F
Fill in the Blanks:
1. ongoing
2. once-and-for-all
3. 4, fall
4. inflation, once-and-for-all
5. money supply, output
6. 7
7. falls, undershoots, steady-state

Problem: (a) 7% p.a. (b) 13% p.a. (c) 6% p.a. (d) jumps from 10% p.a. to 13% p.a. and stays there (e) remains at 7% p.a. (f) rises gradually to overshoot its new steady-state rate of 6% p.a. then slowly falls back to 6% p.a.

CHAPTER 13

U.S. MACROECONOMIC HISTORY: HOW WELL IS IT EXPLAINED BY THE BASIC MODEL?

By now you will have a good understanding of how the basic model determines the levels of real variables (output, employment, unemployment, and real wages) and how it determines the price level, the inflation rate and the rate of interest. You will also know quite a lot about the actual behavior of most of these variables in the United States over the past eighty years. When you have completed your study of this chapter you will know which facts the basic model does explain well and which facts it does not explain. That is you will:

(a) Know the facts that the basic model seeks to explain.
(b) Know the predictions of the basic model.
(c) Know the main labor market shocks in the United States and their effects.
(d) Know the main movements in the growth rate of the money supply and its effects.
(e) Understand what the basic model does and does not explain.

Chapter Summary

A. The Facts

The dominant facts of U.S. macroeconomic history that the basic model seeks to understand are as follows: (1) Inflation, unemployment, and output all fluctuated much more before World War II than afterwards, and interest rate movements have been much smoother than fluctuations in these other three variables. (2) Unemployment displayed a gentle upward trend after World War II, whereas inflation displayed a downward trend in the 1950s but an upward trend in the 1960s and 1970s. (3) Unemployment and output are strongly countercyclical; inflation and unemployment move in opposite directions two-thirds of the time and in the same direction one-third of the time.

B. Predictions of the Basic Model

The basic model predicts that movements in output and unemployment will be caused by labor market shocks induced either by minimum wage laws, labor union actions, unemployment insurance programs, or other government tax changes. Inflation and interest rates will be determined by the growth rate of the money supply. Changes in the growth rate of the money supply will have no effects on the real variables--output, employment, and unemployment.

C. Labor Market Shocks

Minimum wages were introduced in 1938 and have increased in spurts over the period since then. Labor unions have never represented more than a quarter of the U.S. labor force and have, since 1953, represented a declining fraction. Unemployment insurance benefits, expressed as the fraction of earnings replaced, have been remarkably constant over the period since the late 1930s and have provided unemployed workers with a benefit rate in the neighborhood of one-third of average weekly earnings. The coverage of programs has increased dramatically, however, from less than one-third in 1938 to more than four-fifths by the late 1970s. The tax wedge has gradually increased over the postwar years but was remarkably small prior to World War II.

Only one of these labor market shocks, increased coverage of the unemployment insurance programs, seems capable of accounting for the trend observed in the rate of unemployment, and none of them seems capable of accounting for the cycles.

D. Growth and Inflation

Variations in the growth rate of M1 have been remarkably closely related to variations in U.S. inflation. These cycles and broad trends in inflation are well-explained by cycles and trends in money supply growth. The only period when there was a marked departure between the two variables occurred during and immediately after World War II, when wartime price controls bottled up an inflation that was only allowed to unwind at the end of the war.

E. What the Basic Model Does and Does Not Explain

The basic model explains movements in the rate of inflation and explains the existence of, and postwar trend rise in, unemployment. The model does not explain the fluctuations in output and unemployment, nor the persistent tendency for inflation to be related to changes in these real variables. Further, the model does not capture the facts about the relationship between inflation and interest rates.

Multiple Choice

1. a. Unemployment in the United States trended downwards in the 1950s and upwards in the 1960s and 1970s
   b. Inflation in the United States trended upwards after World War II
   c. Inflation and unemployment move in the same direction about twice as often as they move in opposite directions
   d. Inflation, unemployment, and output all fluctuated much more before World War II than afterwards, and interest rate movements have been much smoother than fluctuations in these other three variables

2. The basic model predicts that:

   a. a rise in the minimum wage creates inflation
   b. interest rates will rise if the growth rate of the money supply is cut
   c. changes in the growth rate of the money supply will have no effect on output, employment, and unemployment
   d. a rise in unemployment insurance benefits create inflation but do not change the level of unemployment

3. a. Minimum wages were introduced in 1938 and have been increased each and every year since then so as to keep the minimum real wage constant

b. Unemployment insurance benefits, expressed as the fraction of earnings replaced, have been remarkably constant since the late 1930s at approximately one-third of the average weekly earnings

c. The fraction of the U.S. labor force that is unionized has increased steadily since 1953

d. The tax wage gradually increased up to World War II but since then has been remarkably steady

4. a. The growth rate of M1 and the inflation rate are not closely related

   b. The money supply growth rate has been positive each and every year since 1920

   c. The money supply growth rate fluctuated with a larger amplitude before World War II than after

   d. Comparing the paths of the money supply growth rate and the inflation rate clearly shows that the money supply growth rate overshoots the rate of inflation

5. The basic model:

   a. explains the co-movements of inflation and unemployment

   b. explains the co-movements of interest rates and inflation

   c. cannot explain the negative co-movements in inflation and unemployment

   d. does not explain movements in the rate of inflation or the postwar trend rise in unemployment

<u>True or False</u>

1. The basic model is an old-fashioned model and as such cannot explain any of the recent co-movements in inflation and unemployment.

2. According to the basic model, interest rates should have been higher than they actually were throughout the decade of the 1970s.

3. The basic model predicts that the rate of inflation equals the difference between the rates of growth of the money supply and output.

4. The basic model explains the relationship between the growth rate of the money supply and the inflation rate during the 1970s.

5. The basic model does explain why unemployment exists and why it has trended upwards.

6. The basic model explains the co-movements of inflation and unemployment in the twentieth century.

7. The path of inflation given the growth rate of M1 could have been predicted by anyone using the basic model.

8. The upward trend in unemployment is accounted for by the rise in the tax wedge.

Fill in the Blanks

1. The basic model is capable of explaining the path of __________ and the __________ of and trend __________ in unemployment.

2. The basic model is unable to explain the fluctuations in __________ and __________.

3. The basic model is __________ of explaining the co-movements between inflation and changes in the real variables __________ and __________.

4. The basic model predicts __________ co-movements between inflation and unemployment.

5. The basic model does __________ the negatively-sloped Phillips curve.

6. The basic model predicts that a rise in the tax wedge leads to __________ employment and __________ unemployment.

Answers

Multiple Choice: 1 d 2 c 3 b 4 c 5 c
True or False: 1 F 2 F 3 F 4 F 5 T 6 T 7 T 8 F
Fill in the Blanks:
1. inflation, existence, rise
2. output, unemployment
3. incapable, unemployment, output
4. independent
5. not predict
6. lower, higher

CHAPTER 14

INTRODUCTION TO THE KEYNESIAN MODEL

You now know the basic model of output, employment, and the price level and also know that there is a good deal of our recent macroeconomic history that the basic model cannot explain. You also know the features of the business cycle that the basic model is capable of explaining. In the 1930s John Maynard Keynes modified the basic model. This new model is called the Keynesian model. When you have completed your study of this chapter you will:

(a) Know why you are studying the Keynesian model.
(b) Know the main strengths and weaknesses of the Keynesian model.

Chapter Summary

A. Why Study the Keynesian Model

You are studying the Keynesian model for three reasons:

1. It is the model that governs the thinking of those in positions of authority and power today and is the basis of most current macroeconomic policymaking.
2. It provides the only available, if rudimentary, explanation of the phenomenon of the Great Depression.
3. It contains some modifications to the basic theory of aggregate demand that have been absorbed into the mainstream body of macroeconomics.

B. Strengths and Weaknesses of the Keynesian Model

The main strength of the Keynesian model is that it provides a rudimentary explanation of the Great Depression.

The main weakness of the Keynesian model is that the explanation of the Great Depression which it provides seems to be inconsistent with the notion that individuals and firms seek to maximize utility and profits.

CHAPTER 15

THE KEYNESIAN THEORY OF AGGREGATE SUPPLY

When you have completed your study of this chapter you will:

(a) Know Keynes's modification to the basic model's theory of aggregate supply.
(b) Understand the nature of the Keynesian aggregate supply curve.
(c) Know how to derive the Keynesian aggregate supply curve.
(d) Understand the approximate Keynesian aggregate supply curve--the increase "L".

Chapter Summary

A. Keynes's Modification of the Basic Model

The major modification of the basic model suggested by Keynes was that of replacing the assumption that at all times the labor market achieves an equilibrium where the demand for, and the supply of labor are equal, with the assumption that the money wage is downwardly rigid. The money wage will rise to achieve an equality between the demand and supply if there is an excess demand for labor. The money wage will not fall if there is an excess supply of labor. Instead, the economy gets stuck with a real wage which is too high and with a level of employment which is below the quantity of labor supplied. There is unemployment in such a situation.

B. Keynesian Aggregate Supply Curve

The Keynesian aggregate supply curve, like that in the basic model, shows the maximum amount of output that the economy will supply at each different price level. If the price level is high enough to ensure that the real wage is not above the full-employment real wage, the Keynesian aggregate supply curve is identical to that in the basic model. At price levels below that, however, when the real wage is "too high", the Keynesian aggregate supply curve is derived entirely from the demand for labor by profit-maximizing firms and is not influenced by households' labor supply decisions.

C. How to Derive the Keynesian Aggregate Supply Curve

The Keynesian aggregate supply curve is derived in a four-part analysis which links the demand for labor by profit-maximizing firms through the production function to the quantity of output that will be supplied at each price level. The derivation is presented in the textbook in Figure 15.2 (p. 201) and should be fully understood.

D. Approximate Keynesian Aggregate Supply Curve - The Inverse "L"

The inverse "L" approximation to the Keynesian aggregate supply curve presumes that it is the price level rather than the money wage which is downwardly rigid. This gives a horizontal segment to the aggregate supply curve at the fixed price level up to full-employment output, and then gives a vertical segment at the full-employment level of output.

The important implication of the Keynesian aggregate supply curve (made most clear in the inverse "L" approximate case) is that below full employment, the quantity of output and employment are determined by aggregate demand alone and do not in any way depend on the aggregate supply conditions since the aggregate supply curve itself is horizontal (or nearly so).

Multiple Choice

1. In the Keynesian model:

   a. the real wage is constant
   b. real wages can rise but they do not fall
   c. money wages are constant
   d. money wages adjust quickly so that there is always full employment

2. The Keynesian aggregate supply curve is:

   a. the same as the basic model's aggregate supply curve
   b. horizontal
   c. approximately an inverse "L"
   d. upward sloping

3. a. If there is unemployment the amount of unemployment is directly related to the level of aggregate demand
   b. If there is full employment, the level of output is determined by the level of aggregate demand
   c. If as aggregate demand rises the price level rises, the amount of unemployment is determined by the level of aggregate demand
   d. Technological improvements reduce the amount of unemployment and move the economy closer to full employment

4. In the Keynesian model:

   a. a rise in aggregate demand always cuts the level of unemployment
   b. a rise in aggregate demand does not lead to a change in the level of unemployment
   c. a rise in the price level leads to a drop in unemployment
   d. a rise in aggregate demand raises the price level only if there is full employment

5. In the Keynesian model:

   a. firms do not maximize profits
   b. households always maximize utility as the money wage never falls
   c. firms always maximize profits and households always maximize utility
   d. when there is unemployment households are not maximizing utility

6. A rise in the price level:

   a. shifts the aggregate supply curve to the left
   b. increases the real wage
   c. does not change the money wage
   d. raises the money wage

True or False

1. In the Keynesian model unemployment arises because improvements in technology that are labor-saving displace workers.

2. Unemployment is created in the Keynesian model because the fixed money wage encourages more people to join the labor force.

3. The money wage is fixed in the Keynesian model.

4. A rise in the price level leads to a cut in the demand for goods as they become more expensive. This leads to a rise in unemployment in the Keynesian model.

5. If there is a drought and aggregate supply declines, then the level of unemployment might rise or it could stay the same.

6. Unemployment increases in the Keynesian model when the money wage rises because as the money wage rises firms employ fewer people but more people are encouraged to work.

7. In the Keynesian model, if there is unemployment, households do not maximize utility but firms do maximize profits.

8. Keynes's assumption of downwardly-rigid money wages is a very realistic assumption as no worker would willingly take a job at a lower wage.

Fill in the Blanks

1. Keynes replaced the assumption of the basic model that the ___________ wage adjusts all the time so that the labor market is always in equilibrium, with the assumption that ___________ wage is ___________ rigid.

2. If the labor market is initially at equilibrium and the price level falls, the ___________ wage remains constant and the ___________ wage rises. The labor market is no longer in ___________ and the number of people employed is determined by the ___________ for labor.

3. If the labor market is initially at equilibrium and the price level rises, the ___________ wage rises and by the same percentage as the rise in the ________________ .

4. The Keynesian aggregate supply curve is approximately ___________ .

5. Along the horizontal part of the aggregate supply curve the labor market is ________________ , but along the vertical part there is ___________ in the labor market.

6. When the AD curve cuts the horizontal part of the KAS curve it determines the level of ___________ , but when AD cuts the vertical part of the KAS curve it determines the ______________ .

Problems

1. For a Keynesian economy in which there are 1,000 identical firms the production function is

$$y = 20n - 0.1n^2$$

The labor supply curve is

$$n^s = 5(W/P)$$

The labor demand curve is

$$n^d = 100 - 5(W/P)$$

The price level is

$$P = 2 .$$

At full employment calculate:

(a) the employment level
(b) the money wage

If the price level rises to 3 calculate:

(c) the real wage
(d) the employment level
(e) aggregate supply
(f) the money wage

If the price level falls from 2 to $1\frac{2}{3}$ calculate:

(g) the real wage
(h) the employment level
(i) aggregate supply
(j) the money wage

The Keynesian aggregate supply curve is an inverse "L":

(k) what is the equation to the horizontal portion of the KAS curve?
(ℓ) what is the equation to the vertical portion?

2. An economy has 1,000 competitive firms. Each firm has the following production function:

employment	1	2	3	4	5	6	7	8	9	10
output	11	26	36	44	51	57	62	66	69	71

The supply of labor is given by:

real wage	1	2	3	4	5	6	7	8	9	10
no. of men	0	500	1000	2000	3000	4000	5000	6000	7000	8000

If the money wage is $10 calculate the full-employment level of:

(a) employment
(b) real wage
(c) output

If the price level rose to $4, calculate the Keynesian model predictions of:

(d) the level of output
(e) the level of employment

If the money wage is $10 and the price level fell to $1, calculate the Keynesian model predictions of:

(f) the level of employment
(g) the level of output
(h) the rise in unemployment

Answers

Multiple Choice: 1 b 2 c 3 a 4 d 5 d 6d
True or False: 1 F 2 F 3 F 4 F 5 T 6 F 7 T 8 F
Fill in the Blanks:
1. money, money, downwardly
2. money, real, equilibrium, demand
3. money, price level
4. an inverse L
5. not in equilibrium, equilibrium
6. output, price level

Problems: 1. (a) 50,000 (b) 20 (c) 10 (d) 50,000 (e) 750,000 (f) 30 (g) 12 (h) 40,000 (i) 640,000 (j) 20 (k) P = 2 (ℓ) y = 750,000
2. (a) 5,000 (b) 7 (c) 51,000 (d) 51,000 (e) 5,000 (f) 3,000 (g) 36,000 (h) 5,000

CHAPTER 16

AGGREGATE DEMAND IN THE KEYNESIAN MODEL

When you have completed your study of this chapter you will:

(a) Know the components of aggregate demand.
(b) Know the theories of the consumption function proposed by Keynes, Friedman and Modigliani.
(c) Understand the connection between wealth and income and why current income is a major determinant of consumption.
(d) Know how to represent the consumption and savings functions in simple equations and diagrams.
(e) Understand the Keynesian cross model.

Chapter Summary

A. Components of Aggregate Demand

The components of aggregate demand are consumption, investment, government purchases of goods and services, and net exports.

B. Theories of the Consumption Function Proposed by Keynes, Friedman and Modigliani

Keynes hypothesized that the major determinant of consumption was current disposable income. Keynes supposed that the level of consumption would rise as income rose, but the fraction of income consumed would decline. Friedman and Modigliani developed the permanent income and life-cycle hypotheses, which emphasized the role of wealth as the ultimate constraint upon consumption.

C. Connection Between Wealth and Income and Why Current Income is a Major Determinant of Consumption

Wealth is the present value of current and future income. By borrowing and lending, it is possible to break the direct connection between current income and current consumption. Nevertheless, current income is an important indicator of potential future income and therefore will influence the extent to which an individual can borrow against future labor income and will influence the individual's own assessment of what represents a desirable, sustainable consumption and savings plan. Therefore, current income is a major determinant of consumption.

D. Consumption and Savings Functions in Simple Equations and Diagrams

The consumption function may be written as

$$c = a + b(y-t)$$

Since savings plus consumption must equal disposable income, it follows that the savings function must be

$$s = -a + (1-b)(y-t)$$

If savings and consumption are added together, these always add up to disposable income (y-t).

E. The Keynesian Cross Model

The essence of the simple Keynesian theory of aggregate demand can be summarized in the Keynesian cross diagram. Aggregate demand is measured on the vertical axis and actual output on the horizontal axis. The 45° line says that the level of actual output will equal the quantity demanded. The aggregate demand curve plotted in that diagram shows the consumption function plus the assumed fixed level of investment and government expenditure. The point where the aggregate demand line cuts the 45° line determines the equilibrium level of income. It is an equilibrium in the sense that it is the only income level that generates a level of consumption which, when added to investment and government spending, equals the same level of income.

A rise in investment or government spending (or a cut in taxes) will shift the aggregate demand curve upwards and produce a higher equilibrium income level. The rise in income will be equal to the rise in investment or government expenditure multiplied by $1/(1-b)$, where b is the marginal propensity to consume. A rise in taxes will change income by $-b/(1-b)$ times the rise in taxes (i.e., a tax rise will lower income).

Multiple Choice

1. Aggregate demand is the sum of:

   a. consumption and investment
   b. consumption plus investment plus government spending
   c. consumption plus investment plus government expenditure minus taxes
   d. all expenditures in the economy

2. Consumption expenditure:

   a. is a constant
   b. increases with disposable income
   c. is independent of the level of taxes
   d. falls as government expenditure rises

3. Savings:

   a. are always positive or zero
   b. can be positive, negative or zero as they depend only on gross income
   c. can be below zero
   d. fall as government expenditure rises

4. The slope of the savings function:

   a. is the same as the slope of the consumption function
   b. is at least as big as the slope of the consumption function
   c. is the reciprocal of the slope of the consumption function
   d. plus the consumption function is always 1

5. a. Real income is determined by the level of aggregate demand
   b. As government expenditure rises the equilibrium output level falls
   c. Autonomous spending does not influence the level of real income
   d. A simultaneous rise in government expenditure and taxes which are of the same magnitude do not raise equilibrium real income

True or False

1. When savings rise, consumption falls by the same amount as that by which savings rose.

2. If the marginal propensity to consume is 0.75, then the savings function is steeper than the consumption function.

3. If the marginal propensity to consume is 0.75, the multiplier on autonomous spending is 4.

4. If the marginal propensity to consume is 0.75, the government spending multiplier is 5.

5. If the marginal propensity to consume is 0.75 and there is a balanced budget rise of 100, then real income rises by 75.

6. If the marginal propensity to consume is 0.75 and taxes rise by 100, real income falls by 300.

7. If investment rises by 100, real income rises by 100 divided by the marginal propensity to save.

8. If taxes rise by 100, both consumption and savings fall.

9. If the marginal propensity to consume is 0.8 and taxes rise by 50, consumption falls by 40.

10. If the marginal propensity to consume is 0.8 and taxes rise by 50, savings fall by 40.

Fill in the Blanks

1. The components of aggregate demand are:

   (i) ____________________ (ii) ____________________

   (iii) ____________________ (iv) ____________________

2. ____________ is the major determinant of current consumption.

3. The sum of savings and consumption is __________.

4. The autonomous spending multiplier is __________.

5. The taxation multiplier is __________.

Problems

1. You are given the following information about a hypothetical economy:

   $c = 100 + 0.75(y-t)$

   $i = 500$

   $g = 400,\ t = 400$

   There is unemployment and the price level is fixed.

   (c is consumption, y is real income, t is taxes, i is investment, and g is government expenditure on final goods and services)

   Calculate:

   (a) equilibrium real income
   (b) equilibrium consumption
   (c) the government's budget deficit

   If government expenditure is cut to 300, calculate:

   (d) the change in real income
   (e) the change in consumption
   (f) the change in the government's budget deficit
   (g) the multiplier

   Assume the initial level of government expenditure ($g = 400$) and the government implements a balanced budget cut of 100. Calculate:

   (h) the change in real income
   (i) the change in consumption
   (j) the multiplier

2. If in the above problem the level of taxes is not 400 but increases with income such that the level of taxes is $0.15y$, what now are the answers to the questions (a) to (g) above?

Project

In your university library find the latest issue of The National Income and Product Accounts of the United States (Washington, D.C.: U.S. Department of Commerce) and collect the following data for the years since 1970. (To bring the series right up to date you may have to use the Survey of Current Business):

(i) real consumption
(ii) real GNP
(iii) real disposable income

Using graph paper construct two scatter diagrams. In the first plot real consumption on the vertical axis and real GNP on the horizontal, and in the second plot real consumption on the vertical axis and real disposable income on the horizontal. Draw the best straight line you can through the middle of each scatter diagram.

(a) What is consumption when income is zero?
(b) What are the parameters (a and b) of the consumption function?
(c) Are the slopes of these two lines the same? If they are, what can you conclude; if they are not, what can you conclude?

Answers

Multiple Choice: 1 b 2 b 3 c 4 d 5 a
True or False: 1 F 2 T 3 T 4 F 5 F 6 T 7 T 8 T 9 T 10 F
Fill in the Blanks:
1. consumption, investment, government purchases, net exports
2. current income
3. disposable income
4. 1/(1-b)
5. -b/(1-b)

Problems: 1. (a) 2800 (b) 1900 (c) 0 (d) -400 (e) -300 (f) 100 (g) 4 (h) -100 (i) -75 (j) 1
2. (a) 2758.6 (b) 1858.62 (c) -13.8 (d) -275.9 (e) -175.9 (f) -58.6 (g) 2.76

CHAPTER 17

INVESTMENT DEMAND

When you have completed your study of this chapter you will:

(a) Understand the distinction between investment and the capital stock.
(b) Understand what determines the demand for capital.
(c) Understand what is meant by the rental rate of capital.
(d) Understand how investment demand is related to the demand for capital.
(e) Know how to represent the investment demand function in a simple equation and diagram.

Chapter Summary

A. Distinction Between Investment and Capital Stock

Investment demand is the demand for capital goods for use in production or consumption yielding activities. It represents additions to the stock of capital or the replacement of depreciated capital. Thus, investment is the flow which augments or maintains the stock of capital.

B. The Demand for Capital

The demand for capital is determined by cost-minimizing or profit-maximizing considerations. Capital will be demanded up to the point at which its marginal product equals its rental rate.

C. Rental Rate of Capital

Where capital equipment is explicitly rented, as is often the case with houses, and occasionally with cars, TV sets and industrial equipment, the rental rate of capital is simply the rate per hour that has to be paid for the use of a particular type of equipment. Most capital is not rented explicitly but is owned by the individual or firm that uses it. In such a case, the rental rate on capital is implicit. The individual implicitly rents the equipment from him/herself. That implicit rental rate will be equal to the rate of depreciation plus the market rate of interest (nominal rate of interest) minus the rate of appreciation of the asset in question.

D. Investment and the Demand for Capital

The rate of investment will be determined by the size of the capital stock relative to the profit-maximizing capital stock. The bigger the stock of capital relative to the desired stock, the slower will be the rate of investment. Since the capital stock is a slowly changing variable, as an approximation, the rate of investment may be presumed to depend only on the rental rate of capital. The rental rate will in turn depend primarily upon the real rate of interest. Thus, the simple macroeconomic theory of investment is that it depends upon the real rate of interest. A higher real rate of interest will induce a lower rate of investment. This theory leaves out more than it includes. What is left out, however, may be presumed to be independent of (exogenous with respect to) the other variables that macroeconomics seeks to understand. It is fluctuations in those other variables, however, which are responsible for some of the major swings in investment activity.

E. Investment Demand Function

The investment demand function can be written in a simple equation

$$i = i_0 - hr$$

This equation states that as the real rate of interest, r, rises, the level of investment, i, falls. The constant, h, is the degree of responsiveness of investment to interest rate changes. Volatility of investment is reflected in changes in i_0 that shift the investment demand function.

Multiple Choice

1. Investment is:

    a. the amount of capital in the economy
    b. a stock
    c. the replacement of worn-out capital
    d. neither a stock nor a flow

2. The term rental rate:

    a. is just a fancy name for rent
    b. is the opportunity cost of owning capital
    c. is the interest rate paid on money borrowed from the bank in order to buy capital
    d. includes depreciation costs but not appreciation of the value of the capital

3. The real rental rate is:

    a. the real interest rate
    b. the opportunity cost of owning a piece of capital after taking into account inflation
    c. dependent upon the size of the capital stock
    d. lower, the larger the capital stock

4. a. The demand for capital rises as the rate of depreciation of capital rises
    b. If interest rates rise at the same rate as inflation, the demand for capital falls
    c. If inflation rises faster than interest rates, the demand for capital shifts to the right
    d. If inflation falls faster than interest rates, firms would prefer a smaller capital stock

5. a. The quantity of capital is a stock and one flow that changes that stock is investment
   b. Investment is a stock and it is depreciation that changes that stock
   c. Depreciation is a technologically given constant and as such is a stock and not a flow
   d. Net investment is the flow which, along with depreciation, changes the stock of investment

True or False

1. Investment depends on the relationship between the actual capital stock and that which is desired. It has nothing to do with the interest rate.

2. If the actual stock of capital equals the desired stock, investment is zero.

3. An increase in consumption expenditure leads to an increase in the demand for capital and thus raises investment.

4. The higher the real interest rate, the smaller is the desired capital stock and therefore the lower is the rate of investment.

5. The smaller the actual capital stock, the larger is the rate of investment.

6. Changes in the rate of interest either raise or lower the rate of investment, but they do not shift the investment demand function.

7. As entrepreneurs' perceptions of profit opportunities change, swings in the investment demand function are generated.

8. Volatility in investment demand arises from such things as changes in technology and not changes in the real rental rate of capital.

Fill in the Blanks

1. Investment is a __________, capital is a __________, and depreciation of capital is a __________.

2. The stock of capital is determined so as to minimize __________ or maximize __________. Capital is demanded up to the point where its __________ equals its __________.

3. The rate of investment is determined by the relationship between __________ capital stock and ______________________________ capital stock.

4. __________ depends on the rental rate but the rental rate, in turn, depends on _________________________.

Problems

1. A car which you are thinking of buying costs $5000 and will, after one year, have a resale value of $4500. The rate of interest on the bank loan which you would take out if you did buy the car is 12% per annum. A friend who already owns an identical car offers to lease you his car for one year at $1200 (you buy the gas and pay for the maintenance).

   (a) Should you lease from your friend or should you buy the car?
   (b) What is the rental rate that your friend is asking?
   (c) What is the implicit rental rate if you buy the car?
   (d) What is the real rental rate that you would be paying in (a)?

2. A firm decides to buy a piece of equipment rather than lease it for $10,000 per annum. The market interest rate paid by the firm on the loan is 10% and the rate of increase of the price of this equipment is 7%. The equipment depreciates at the rate of 10% per annum.

   (a) Over what range of prices would the firm be willing to buy the equipment?
   (b) What is the implicit rental rate that would make the firm indifferent between buying and leasing?
   (c) If inflation and the market interest rate both rose by one percentage point, how does your answer to (b) change?
   (d) If inflation increases and rises faster than the market interest rate, how does your answer to (b) change?

Project

In your university library, find the latest issue of National Income and Product Accounts of the United States (Washington, D.C.: U.S. Department of Commerce) and collect data on private investment since 1970. From the data sources given in the Appendix to Chapter 2 of the textbook (pp. 27-29) collect the long-term interest rate and the GNP deflator since 1970. Construct two series, (i) real private investment by dividing private investment by the GNP deflator, and (ii) the real interest rate by dividing the long-term interest rate by the GNP deflator

Using graph paper construct a scatter diagram by plotting the real interest rate on the horizontal axis and real private investment on the vertical axis. Draw the best straight line that you can through the points of the scatter diagram. What are the values of the parameters of the investment function? What is the equation to the investment function?

Answers

Multiple Choice: 1 c 2 b 3 b 4 d 5 a
True or False: 1 F 2 F 3 T 4 T 5 T 6 T 7 T 8 T
Fill in the Blanks:
1. flow, stock, flow
2. costs, profits, marginal product, rental rate
3. actual, profit maximizing
4. investment, real rate of interest

Problems:
1. (a) buy (b) $1200 (c) $1100 (d) 0.22
2. (a) < $76,923.1 (b) 13.0 (c) no change (d) rises

CHAPTER 18

THE IS CURVE

By the time you have completed your study of this chapter you will:

(a) Know the definition of the IS curve.
(b) Know how to derive the IS curve.
(c) Understand what determines the slope of the IS curve.
(d) Understand what makes the IS curve shift and by how much.

Chapter Summary

A. Definition of the IS Curve

The IS curve is the relationship between the aggregate demand for goods and services and the real rate of interest when flow equilibrium prevails in the goods market, that is, when investment-plus-government spending is equal to planned savings-plus-taxes.

B. Derivation of the IS Curve

The IS curve is derived from the investment-plus-government spending curve, the planned savings-plus-taxes curve, and the equality of investment-plus-government spending and savings-plus-taxes. Figures 18.1 through 18.4 in the textbook (pp. 242-46) illustrate this and should be thoroughly understood.

C. Determinants of the IS Curve Slope

The IS curve slopes downwards. That is, at lower real interest rates higher levels of real income are required to maintain flow equilibrium in the goods market. This arises because, at lower interest rates, there is more investment spending, and with higher investment there needs to be higher savings to maintain equilibrium. Higher savings require a higher level of income, so that lower interest rates require higher income levels. More precisely, the slope of the IS curve is equal to the slope of the investment demand curve multiplied by (1-b) where b is the marginal propensity to consume.

D. Shifts in the IS Curve

The IS curve shifts when government spending and taxes change. A rise in government spending will lead to a rightward shift in the IS curve by an amount equal to 1/(1-b) times the change in government spending. A rise in taxes will cause the IS curve to shift leftwards. The amount of the shift will be equal to the rise in taxes times b/(1-b).

Multiple Choice

1. a. Along the IS curve investment always equals savings
   b. Along the IS curve there is flow equilibrium in the markets for all goods produced in the economy
   c. In the closed economy, consumption plus government spending always equals savings plus taxes
   d. Savings plus taxes equals investment plus government spending all along the IS curve, if international trade in goods is balanced

2. a. The IS curve and the investment function are both positively sloped. Their slopes are the same
   b. If the marginal propensity to consume rises, the IS curve becomes steeper
   c. If the government taxed people according to their incomes rather than at a flat rate per person, the IS curve would be flatter
   d. If the responsiveness of investment to interest rates rose, the IS curve would become flatter

3. a. A rise in government expenditure accompanied by a cut in taxes shifts the IS curve to the right
   b. A balanced budget rise in government expenditure does not shift the IS curve
   c. A rise in taxes shifts the IS curve upwards
   d. A rise in government spending financed by the sale of bonds does not shift the IS curve

4. a. The IS curve cannot be horizontal. It is positively sloped
   b. The more responsive investment is to changes in the interest rate, the steeper is the IS curve
   c. If investment is independent of the interest rate, the IS curve is horizontal
   d. If investment is elastic with respect to the interest rate, then the IS curve is horizontal

5. a. If people decide to save more, such that the savings function shifts upwards, then the IS curve shifts to the right
   b. If the government taxed people according to their income, then the lower the rate of tax, the flatter the IS curve
   c. If people never save and the government levies a constant amount of tax per person, the IS curve is identical to the investment function
   d. If the government levies no taxes but pays for its spending by selling bonds, the IS curve would be horizontal

True or False

1. A rise in government expenditure raises the demand for goods and shifts the IS curve to the right by the amount of the rise in government expenditure.

2. If the government raises taxes, people cut their consumption expenditure. If the government spends the additional tax revenue then the total demand for goods remains the same and therefore the IS curve does not shift.

3. If the marginal propensity to consume rises, the IS curve becomes flatter.

4. If government spending rises by 100 when the marginal propensity to consume is 0.75, the IS curve shifts to the right by 400.

5. If taxes fall by 50 when the marginal propensity to save is 0.25, the IS curve shifts to the right by 105.

Fill in the Blanks

1. IS curve is the relationship between ________________ for ___________ goods and services and the ___________ rate of interest when ___________ equilibrium prevails in the goods market.

2. Along the IS curve in a closed economy ___________ plus government spending always equals ___________ plus taxes.

3. The IS curve is ___________ sloped and the slope is equal to ___________.

4. The IS curve will shift if there is a change in (i) ____________________________ or (ii) ___________ .

5. The IS curve shifts to the right if (i) ______________________ increases or (ii) ___________ decreases.

6. A balanced budget rise in government spending shifts the IS curve ___________ by the amount ___________________________________.

Problems

1. You are given the following information about a hypothetical economy:

   1. $c = 100 + 0.75(y - t)$
   2. $i = 500 - 25r$
   3. $g = 300,\ t = 300$

   where c is consumption, i is investment, r is the interest rate expressed as a percentage, g is government spending and t is taxes.

   (a) What is the equation to the IS curve?
   (b) What is the slope of the IS curve?
   (c) If government expenditure rises by 100, what is the change in income?
   (d) If taxes rise by 100, what is the change in income?
   (e) If both government spending and taxes rise by 100, what is the change in income?
   (f) If investment becomes more responsive to changes in the interest rate, how does the IS curve change?
   (g) What is the slope of the investment function?

(h) Compare the slopes of the IS curve and the investment function. Which is flatter?

(i) If the rate of interest was a constant 5%, what is the level of income?

(j) If the rate of interest falls from 5% to 4%, what is the change in the level of income?

2. If, in the above example, the government levies taxes at the rate of 20% of income, what now are the answers to the questions (a) to (c) above?

Answers

Multiple Choice: 1 d 2 d 3 a 4 d 5 b

True or False: 1 F 2 F 3 T 4 T 5 T

Fill in the Blanks:

1. aggregate demand, final, real, flow
2. investment, savings
3. negatively, $-(1-b)/h$
4. government spending, taxes
5. government spending, taxes
6. to the right, of the change in government spending

Problems: 1. (a) $y = 2760 - 100r$ (b) -0.01 (c) 400 (d) -300
(e) 100 (f) flatter (g) -0.04 (h) IS curve (i) 2260 (j) -100

2. (a) $y = 2250 - 62.5r$ (b) -0.016 (c) 250

CHAPTER 19

THE DEMAND FOR MONEY, THE SUPPLY OF MONEY, AND THE LM CURVE

When you have completed your study of this chapter you will:

(a) Know the definition of the LM curve.
(b) Know how to derive the LM curve.
(c) Understand what determines the slope of the LM curve.
(d) Understand what makes the LM curve shift and by how much.

Chapter Summary

A. Definition of the LM Curve

The LM curve is defined as an equilibrium locus that traces out the relationship between the rate of interest and the level of real income when the money supply is equal to the amount of money demanded.

B. Derivation of the LM Curve

The LM curve is derived graphically in the textbook in Figure 19.1 (p. 260). This derivation should be thoroughly understood.

C. Determinants of the LM Curve Slope

The LM curve slopes upwards. That is due to the fact that as the interest rate rises, people economize on their holdings of money. With a given quantity of money in existence, the only way that monetary equilibrium can be obtained at higher interest rates is for there to be a higher level of real income to induce a rise in the demand for money which will offset the economizing on money holdings. The less elastic is the demand for money with respect to the interest rate, the steeper will be the LM curve. Also, the more responsive is the demand for money to income changes, the steeper will be the LM curve.

D. Shifts in the LM Curve

The LM curve will shift if the money supply changes or if the price level changes. A rise in the quantity of money will make the LM curve shift to the right by an amount equal to (1/k) times the rise in the real money supply. A rise in the price level will have an equivalent but opposite effect on the LM curve to that of a rise in the money supply.

Multiple Choice

1. The quantity of real balances that people wish to hold in aggregate:

    a. rises with inflation
    b. varies directly with the real interest rate
    c. varies inversely with the nominal interest rate
    d. does not change with the level of real income

2. a. Along the LM curve output and the price level are such that the money market is in equilibrium
   b. If the money supply is such that the demand for goods equals the supply of goods then the interest rate and the level of real income are such that the economy is on the LM curve
   c. If the level of real income is such that the demand for money equals the supply of money then the interest rate can be read off the LM curve
   d. If the Fed changes the money supply then a movement along the LM curve shows how the interest rate responds

3. a. The LM curve is positively sloped and as such it can range from being horizontal to being vertical
   b. The LM curve is flatter, the more responsive the demand for money is to changes in real income
   c. The LM curve is steeper, the more responsive the demand for money is to changes in the interest rate
   d. A fall in the money supply raises the interest rate and so moves the economy up the LM curve

4. a. A rise in the price level lowers the demand for real balances and so the LM curve shifts to the right
   b. If the demand for money becomes more responsive to changes in the interest rate the LM curve becomes flatter
   c. If the demand for money becomes more responsive to changes in income the LM curve becomes flatter
   d. A fall in the price level does not change the demand for real balances, but in order for the money market to be in equilibrium the supply of money must also fall

5. a. The LM curve is vertical if people do not use notes and coins when making their purchases
   b. The LM curve becomes steeper the larger is the number of people who use a credit card when making their purchases
   c. The LM curve is horizontal if all stores are willing to accept checks as payment for goods bought
   d. The LM curve is horizontal if all stores are willing to accept government bonds (non-money assets) as well as money for goods bought

6. a. If the money supply rises by 100, the LM curve shifts to the right by 100
   b. If the price level doubles, the demand for real balances halves
   c. If the money supply falls, the shift of the LM curve to the left is greater the lower the price level
   d. If the responsiveness of the demand for real balances to a change in income falls, the LM curve becomes steeper

True or False

1. A rise in government expenditure financed by a sale of bonds raises the demand for real balances and so shifts the LM curve.

2. A lowering of the money supply raises the interest rate and moves the economy up the LM curve.

3. A lowering of the money supply shifts the LM curve to the left.

4. When the money supply is raised the price level rises by the same percentage amount so that the LM curve does not move.

5. If the responsiveness of the demand for real balances to a change in income rises the LM curve becomes steeper so that any change in the money supply leads to smaller shifts in the LM curve.

Fill in the Blanks

1. The LM curve is the relationship between the rate of ____________ and the level of ____________ when the ____________ equals the ____________.

2. The LM curve is ____________ sloped. Its slope is equal to ______.

3. A rise in the money supply shifts the LM curve ____________.

4. The less responsive is the demand for money to real income changes, the ____________ will be the LM curve.

5. The ____________ elastic is the demand for money with respect to the interest rate, the flatter will be the LM curve.

Problem

Consider the following hypothetical economy:

1. The demand for real balances rises by 35 for each 1 unit fall in the real rate of interest
2. The demand for real balances is always at least equal to 300
3. The demand for real balances rises by 0.2 for each 1 unit rise in the level of income
4. The stock of money is 1,000
5. The price level is 2

(a) What is the equation to the LM curve?
(b) What is the slope of the LM curve?
(c) If the money supply rises by 100, what is the change in income if the interest rate is constant?
(d) If the money supply rises by 100, what is the change in the slope of the LM curve?
(e) If the price level rises to 2.5, what is the change in income if the interest rate is constant?
(f) If both the money supply and the price level double, what is the change in income if the interest rate is constant?

(g) If the demand for real balances rises by 40, instead of 35, for each 1 unit fall in the real rate of interest, what is now the slope of the LM curve?
(h) If the demand for real balances rises by 0.25, instead of 0.2, for each 1 unit rise in the level of income, what is now the slope of the LM curve?
(i) If money and non-money assets become perfect substitutes, what is now the slope of the LM curve?
(j) If money and non-money assets become independent, what is now the slope of the LM curve?

Project

In your university library, find the latest Economic Report of the President and collect data on the average stock of M1, the average stock of M2 and the (short-term) interest rate paid on commercial paper (6 months) for each year since 1970. Also find the National Income and Product Accounts of the United States (Washington D.C.: U.S. Department of Commerce) and collect GNP since 1970.

Calculate:

(a) M1/GNP
(b) M2/GNP.

Using some graph paper, construct two diagrams. On the vertical axis of each measure the short-term interest rate. On the horizontal axis of the first diagram measure M1/GNP, and on the horizontal axis of the second diagram measure M2/GNP. Plot the two scatter diagrams. Through each scatter diagram draw the best straight line that you can.

What does the slope of each line measure? Compare the slopes of these two lines. Would you expect the slopes to be the same or different? Can you find an explanation of why the slopes are as shown in your graphs?

Answers

Multiple Choice: 1 c 2 c 3 a 4 b 5 d 6 c
True or False: 1 F 2 F 3 T 4 T 5 T
Fill in the Blanks:
1. interest, real income, money supply, money demand
2. positively, k/ℓ
3. to the right
4. flatter
5. more

Problem: (a) $y = 1,000 + 175r$ (b) 0.006 (c) 250 (d) 0 (e) -500 (f) 0 (g) 0.005 (h) 0.007 (i) 0 (j) ∞

CHAPTER 20

EQUILIBRIUM IN THE KEYNESIAN MODEL

When you have completed your study of this chapter you will:

(a) Understand why the intersection of the IS and LM curves determines the equilibrium levels of output and the interest rate in the Keynesian model.
(b) Know the properties of the IS-LM equilibrium.
(c) Understand the effects of changes in government expenditure and taxes in the Keynesian model.
(d) Understand the effects of a change in the money supply in the Keynesian model.
(e) Understand how to interpret the Keynesian model as a more general theory of aggregate demand than that of the basic model.

Chapter Summary

A. Equilibrium at the IS-LM Intersection

Because the price level is fixed in the Keynesian analysis, the level of output is determined purely by the level of aggregate demand. The IS curve shows the level of income at each level of the interest rate, which equates savings-plus-taxes with investment-plus-government spending. The LM curve gives another relationship between income and the interest rate, which equates the supply of and the demand for money. There is just one level of the interest rate and of income at which both of these relationships are simultaneously satisfied. This point is the equilibrium of the Keynesian model.

B. Properties of the IS-LM Equilibrium

The IS-LM equilibrium occurs when both the demand for money equals the supply of money and when savings-plus-taxes equals investment-plus-government spending. It is assumed that the forces making for equality of both those sets of magnitudes are strong enough to ensure that the economy is never observed away from equilibrium. If savings-plus-taxes were to exceed investment-plus-government spending, real income would fall quickly enough and far enough to restore the equality. If the demand for money exceeded the supply of money, the act of attempting to reduce money balances and acquire bonds would put downward pressure on interest rates to the point at which the amount of money in existence was willingly held. Both sets of forces will occur sufficiently quickly for the economy never to be observed "off" either the IS or LM curves. Thus, the intersection point of the IS and LM curves is the point that describes the state of the economy.

C. Changes in Government Expenditure and Taxes

In general, a rise in government spending or a cut in taxes will raise the level of real income and raise the rate of interest. The steeper the IS curve, the greater will be the rise in both variables. The flatter the LM curve, the greater will be the rise in real income and the smaller will be the rise in the interest rate.

D. Changes in the Money Supply

In general, a rise in the money supply will lead to a rise in real income and a fall in the rate of interest. The steeper the LM curve the larger will be the change in both variables. The flatter the IS curve the greater will be the change in real income and the smaller will be the change in interest rate.

E. The Keynesian Model as a General Theory of Aggregate Demand

Although there is no need to derive a Keynesian aggregate demand curve for the purposes of conducting Keynesian analysis, such an aggregate demand curve is implied by the Keynesian theory. By hypothetically varying the price level, a Keynesian aggregate demand curve may be traced out. Like that of the basic model, the Keynesian aggregate demand curve will be downward sloping. In general, the aggregate demand curve will shift when the money stock changes, when government spending changes, or when taxes change. There are special extreme cases in which some of the variables under government control have no effect on the aggregate demand curve. If the IS curve is vertical or the LM curve is horizontal, only government spending and taxes shift the aggregate demand curve; changes in the money supply leave the curve unaffected. This is the Keynesian cross model. At the other extreme, if the IS curve is horizontal or the LM curve is vertical, then changes in the money supply will shift the aggregate demand curve, but changes in government spending and taxes will leave it unaffected. This is the basic model.

Multiple Choice

1. a. In the Keynesian model if the economy is at the intersection of the IS and LM curves it is in equilibrium, despite the fact that there is unemployment
   b. If the economy is "off" the IS curve the goods market is not cleared so the price level adjusts to move the economy back to equilibrium
   c. If the economy is "off" the LM curve the central bank automatically adjusts the money supply to move the economy back onto the LM curve
   d. If there is unemployment the demand for goods must exceed the supply of goods so that the economy is at equilibrium only if there exists no unemployment

2. Equilibrium in the Keynesian model occurs where:

   a. the demand for money equals the supply of money and savings equals investment
   b. the government budget is balanced, savings equals investment, and the money market is in equilibrium
   c. consumption plus government spending plus investment equals output and the demand for money equals the supply of money
   d. savings plus government spending equals taxes plus investment and the money market is in equilibrium

3. a. If there is a rise in government expenditure financed by an increase in taxes there is no change in either the interest rate or the level of income
   b. If there is a rise in government expenditure financed by an increase in taxation then both the interest rate and real income rise
   c. If an increase in government expenditure is financed by money printing then the interest rate falls and real income rises
   d. If government expenditure rises and it is financed by a sale of bonds the interest rate rises but real income falls

4. a. If the central bank raises the money supply, interest rates rise and investment falls so that aggregate demand for goods and services also falls
   b. If there is a once-and-for-all change in the price level there is no change in the interest rate or in output
   c. The government could lower the interest rate by expanding the money supply but it does this at the risk of creating inflation
   d. A rise in the money supply lowers interest rates and stimulates aggregate demand

5. a. If investment is perfectly elastic with respect to interest rates, expansionary fiscal policy raises both interest rates and output
   b. If the demand for money is completely insensitive to interest rates, expansionary monetary policy does not change interest rates
   c. If money and non-money assets are perfect substitutes, expansionary fiscal policy raises output and employment, but has no effect on interest rates
   d. If investment is independent of interest rates, expansionary monetary or fiscal policy does not change interest rates

True or False

1. The flatter is the IS curve, the larger are all the multipliers.

2. The tax multiplier is always -b times the government expenditure multiplier.

3. Both expansionary monetary policy and expansionary fiscal policy lower unemployment, but they have opposite effects on interest rates.

4. The sizes of the multipliers depend on the slopes of the IS and LM curves.

5. The money multiplier rises from 0 to $1/k$ when the price level is one and the fiscal policy multiplier falls from $1/(1-b)$ to 0, as the ratio h/ℓ goes from 0 to ∞.

6. A balanced-budget rise in government spending always raises real income by the same amount as the rise in government spending.

7. If money and nonmoney assets are regarded as perfect substitutes then expansionary monetary policy lowers interest rates and raises real income.

Fill in the Blanks

1. Because the price level is fixed, the level of real income is determined purely by the level of ________________. Because the IS curve is ____________ sloped and the LM curve is ____________ sloped there is only one rate of ____________ and level of ____________ at which the economy is in equilibrium in the Keynesian model.

2. The intersection of the IS and LM curves is the equilibrium level of output and the level of ____________.

3. The level of aggregate demand rises if there is a rise in ________________________ or ____________ or a fall in ____________.

4. A rise in the money supply ____________ interest rates and ____________ real income. The steeper is the LM curve the ____________ is the change in interest rates and real income.

5. A balanced budget rise in government spending ____________ interest rates and ____________ real income. The flatter is the IS curve the ____________ the interest rate change and the ____________ the real income change.

Problems

1. You are given the following information about a hypothetical economy:

    1. the marginal propensity to consume is 0.8.
    2. private investment falls by 45 for each 1 unit rise in the real interest rate.
    3. the demand for real balances rises by 35 for each 1 unit fall in the real rate of interest.
    4. the amount of personal consumption when income equals taxes is 200.
    5. government spending and taxes are each equal to 500.
    6. the stock of money is 1000.
    7. the amount of private investment is always at most 600.
    8. the demand for real balances is always at least 300.
    9. the demand for real balances rises by 0.2 for each 1 unit rise in the level of income.
    10. the price level is 2.
    11. there is unemployment.

   Calculate:

   (a) the equilibrium real rate of interest
   (b) the equilibrium output
   (c) the equilibrium demand for real balances
   (d) the equilibrium level of consumption
   (e) the equilibrium private investment

Calculate for a balanced budget rise in government spending of 100:

(f) the change in the real interest rate
(g) the change in real income
(h) the balanced budget multiplier on real income if money and non-money assets are perfect substitutes

If investment is perfectly elastic with respect to the interest rate and money and non-money assets are imperfect substitutes calculate:

(i) the money multiplier on real income
(j) the money multiplier on the interest rate
(k) the balanced budget multiplier on real income

2. You are given the following information about a hypothetical economy:

1. $c = 200 + .6(y - t)$
2. $i = 500 - 100r$
3. $g = 300, \ t = 400$
4. $\frac{M^d}{P} = \frac{1}{5}y + 500 - 50r$
5. $M = 700$
6. $P = 1$

Calculate the equilibrium values of:

(a) output
(b) consumption
(c) investment
(d) interest rate

Find the effect on equilibrium income of a unit rise in:

(e) the money supply
(f) government spending
(g) taxes

Answers

Multiple Choice: 1 a 2 c 3 b 4 d 5 c
True or False: 1 F 2 T 3 T 4 T 5 T 6 F 7 F
Fill in the Blanks:
1. aggregate demand, negatively, positively, interest, real income
2. aggregate demand
3. government spending, money supply, taxes
4. lowers, raises, larger
5. raises, raises, smaller, larger

Problems:
1. (a) 8.75 (b) 2531.25 (c) 500 (d) 1825 (e) 206.25 (f) 0.25 (g) 43.75 (h) 1 (i) 2.5 (j) 0 (k) 0
2. (a) 1450 (b) 830 (c) 320 (d) 1.8% (e) 2.5 (f) 1.25 (g) -0.5

CHAPTER 21

THE NEOCLASSICAL SYNTHESIS

When you have completed your study of this chapter you will:

(a) Know what is meant by the term neoclassical synthesis.
(b) Understand how the Keynesian theory of aggregate demand works at full employment when the price level is rising.
(c) Understand the neoclassical theory of price adjustment.
(d) Understand the role of price level expectations in the neoclassical theory of price adjustment and understand the "natural rate" hypothesis.
(e) Understand the explanation of the business cycle given by the neoclassical synthesis.
(f) Understand the policy implications of the neoclassical synthesis.

Chapter Summary

A. Definition of "Neoclassical Synthesis"

The term neoclassical synthesis describes a body of macroeconomic analysis designed to explain the determination of output, prices, employment, and interest rates and to account for the cyclical fluctuations in those variables. It is an amalgamation of the basic model, the Keynesian model, and a gradual price and wage adjustment hypothesis.

B. The Keynesian Theory at Full Employment

The Keynesian theory of aggregate demand, which determines output at less than full employment, becomes a theory of the price level at full employment. It yields all the same predictions as those generated by the basic model. A once-and-for-all rise in the money stock raises the price level proportionately. A continuing rise in the money stock generates an inflation rate that is equal to the growth rate of the money stock (minus the growth rate of output). A rise in the growth rate of the money supply produces a rise in the inflation rate, but the inflation rate overshoots the money supply growth rate en route to the new equilibrium.

C. The Neoclassical Theory of Price Adjustment

The neoclassical theory of price adjustment asserts that prices rise when there is excess demand and fall when there is excess supply. The adjustment process is asymmetrical. A 1 percent excess demand would produce a faster price rise than the price fall that would be generated by a 1 percent excess supply.

D. Inflation Expectations and the "Natural Rate" Hypothesis

Properly understood, the neoclassical theory of price adjustment is a theory of relative price adjustment. Nominal price adjustment will therefore be greater at each and every level of excess demand, one-for-one as the expected inflation rate rises. The expected rate of inflation is a slowly evolving variable, which may be treated as exogenous in the neoclassical analysis.

E. The Neoclassical Explanation of the Business Cycle

The neoclassical synthesis explains the business cycle as the working out of the effects of swings in the aggregate demand curve generated either by shifts in the IS curve or shifts in the LM curve. These shifts themselves arise from changing investment demand, changes in government spending and taxes, and changes in the money supply.

F. Policy Implications of the Neoclassical Synthesis

The neoclassical synthesis implies that by moving government spending, taxes, and the money supply in a manner that offsets the changes in aggregate demand arising from price behavior, the aggregate demand curve can be stabilized, and as a result, so can the level of output, prices, and interest rates.

Multiple Choice

1. The neoclassical synthesis:

   a. is the combination of the basic model and the Keynesian model
   b. explains how output, employment and the interest rate are determined
   c. is the Keynesian model with a wage and price adjustment hypothesis
   d. determines output, prices, employment, the interest rate, and accounts for cyclical fluctuations in each of these variables

2. The Keynesian model at full employment predicts that a rise in the money supply:

   a. will raise the price level in a one-to-one fashion
   b. will raise aggregate demand and therefore raise output with no change in the price level
   c. will raise both the price level and output
   d. will raise interest rates and leave the price level stable

3. The neoclassical theory of price adjustment assumes that:

   a. a 10 percent rise in the price level leads to less than a 10 percent rise in excess demand
   b. 2 percent excess supply leads to prices rising by more than the fall in prices resulting from 2 percent excess demand
   c. 2 percent excess demand leads to a higher rate of inflation than the rate of deflation resulting from 2 percent excess supply
   d. the price level rises with excess demand and falls with excess supply in a one-to-one fashion

4. a. The expectation of inflation has no role in the neoclassical theory of price adjustment
   b. The price adjustment curve suggested by the neoclassical theory of price adjustment shifts downwards as the expectation of inflation rises
   c. The neoclassical theory of price adjustment suggests that the price adjustment curve is just a short-run Phillips curve which shifts each time the expectation of inflation changes. The price adjustment curve shifts such that at the natural rate of unemployment the actual inflation equals that which is expected
   d. Once expected inflation is introduced into the neoclassical theory of price adjustment it becomes a theory of relative prices

5. The business cycle is explained by the neoclassical synthesis as arising from fluctuations in aggregate demand coming solely from:

   a. volatile money supply growth
   b. volatile investment policy
   c. volatility in either the LM or the IS curve
   d. fluctuations in the level of employment

6. a. The business cycle can be avoided by the government adjusting its monetary and fiscal policies so as to offset any volatility in investment demand or consumption demand so as to maintain a steady level of aggregate demand
   b. If the government sets an example by holding its fiscal and monetary policy steady then firms and households will follow suit by keeping their investment demand and consumption demand constant. This would remove the business cycle
   c. The cyclical forces which create the business cycle are so strong that there is no policy which could eliminate the business cycle
   d. Volatility in investment demand sets up the cyclical forces which bring about the business cycle

True or False

1. Swings in the money supply lead to shifts in the aggregate demand curve and the price adjustment curve. It is impossible to trace out a business cycle without shifts in both the aggregate demand and the price adjustment curves.

2. The neoclassical synthesis takes the Keynesian model and adds to it a theory of price adjustment.

3. The theory of price adjustment incorporates a good theory of the expectation of inflation.

4. The neoclassical synthesis is a full-employment analysis. That is, it assumes as its basis the Keynesian model at full employment. Employment is therefore never able to vary from its full-employment level.

5. The neoclassical synthesis tells us that if expectations of inflation rise then inflation itself will rise.

6. Whether the interest rate is procyclical or countercyclical depends upon whether the volatility in the economy is leading to shifts in the IS curve or the LM curve.

Fill in the Blanks

1. The neoclassical synthesis is an amalgamation of (i) _______________, (ii) _______________ and (iii) _______________.

2. A ____________ rise in the money supply in the Keynesian model at full employment generates inflation. The rate of inflation equals _______________.

3. The neoclassical theory of price adjustment assumes that the rise in prices resulting from 10% excess demand is ____________ than the fall in prices resulting from 10% excess supply. The price adjustment curve cuts the vertical axis where _______________ equals _______________.

4. A rise in the expected inflation rate shifts the price adjustment curve ____________. A rise in the natural rate of unemployment shifts the price adjustment curve to the ____________.

5. The business cycle is generated by swings in aggregate ____________ arising from volatility in private demand for ____________ or the _______________ function. The business cycle results from the behavior of private agents. The government can conduct ____________ and ____________ policy so as to offset the swings in aggregate demand and ____________ the business cycle.

Answers

Multiple Choice: 1 d 2 a 3 c 4 c 5 c 6 a
True, False: 1 F 2 F 3 F 4 F 5 T 6 T
Fill in the Blanks:
1. basic model, Keynesian model, price and wage adjustment hypothesis
2. continuous, growth rate of the money supply less the growth rate of output
3. more, actual inflation, expected inflation
4. upwards, left
5. demand, goods, money demand, monetary, fiscal, eliminate

CHAPTER 22

RECENT U.S. ECONOMIC HISTORY: HOW WELL IS IT EXPLAINED BY THE NEOCLASSICAL SYNTHESIS?

When you have completed your study of this chapter you will:

(a) Know the main predictions of the neoclassical model.
(b) Know the way in which the neoclassical model accounts for the Great Depression.
(c) Know how the model explains the high years of neoclassical macroeconomics in the decade from 1958 to 1967.
(d) Know how the model fails to account for the facts in the 1970s.
(e) Understand the main strengths and weaknesses of the neoclassical model.

Chapter Summary

A. Predictions of the Neoclassical Model

The neoclassical model predicts that a shock which shifts the IS curve (expansionary fiscal policy, or a rise in investment spending) will raise interest rates, inflation, and output. After the impact, interest rates will continue to rise, but inflation and output will drift downwards towards their previous values. A rise in the growth rate of the money supply will have no impact effects. It will set up a process, however, of initially falling interest rates, rising inflation, and rising output. Eventually interest rates will also rise to reflect fully the higher inflation. The impact effect of a negative supply side shock will be to raise inflation. The adjustment process will involve rising interest rates, falling inflation, and falling output. The impact effect of a rise in the expected rate of inflation will be to raise inflation, raise output, raise the nominal rate of interest, but cut the real rate of interest. The adjustment process will involve falling inflation and output and rising real and nominal rates of interest. If the rise in inflation expectations was temporary, the economy would eventually return to its initial equilibrium, but inflation and output would undershoot its steady-state values and the real rate of interest would overshoot in the process.

B. A Neoclassical Interpretation of the Great Depression

The onset of the Great Depression is accounted for by the neoclassical model as the result of two simultaneous shocks--a drop in inflation expectations and a cut in the growth rate of the money supply. No shifts in the IS or LM curves necessarily appeared in the first two years. At the depth of the recession, the IS curve shifted to the left as confidence declined, and the LM curve shifted to the left as the real money supply was cut by even tighter monetary policies. At the depth of the depression there was a sharp rise in inflation expectations. The recovery was associated with a restoration of investor confidence, shifting the IS curve to the right, and a strong increase in the money supply, raising real money balances and shifting the LM curve to the right.

C. The Neoclassical Decade: 1958-1967

The neoclassical decade was a period in which inflation expectations appear to have been roughly constant at 2.5% per annum, so that the economy was on a single PA curve. Most of the movements in real income, interest rates, and the actual rate of inflation can be well accounted for by the notion of an IS curve that swung to and fro, generating the cycle in real activity with procyclical co-movements in interest rate and inflation.

D. The 1970s

The major movements in the economy in the 1970s can only be made sense of by supposing that there were sizable shifts (mainly upward) in inflation expectations. No simple neoclassical account of the facts of the 1970s is possible.

E. Strengths and Weaknesses of the Neoclassical Model

The main strengths of the neoclassical model are: (1) its capacity to account for the facts when inflation expectations are constant; and (2) its capacity to provide a framework for analyzing the consequences of changes in inflation expectations.

The main weaknesses of the model are its failure to explain why inflation expectations change and the seeming irrationality in labor supply behavior and in the exogeneity of inflation expectations.

Multiple Choice

1. The neoclassical model predicts that the impact effect of:

   a. a positive shock to the investment function raises employment, raises both the real and nominal rates of interest by the same amount, but that inflation does not change
   b. a positive shock to the money supply growth rate is that interest rates fall, and both output and inflation rise
   c. a negative supply side shock is that excess demand is created in all markets so that wages, interest rates, and inflation all rise
   d. a drop in private consumption demand is that interest rates, inflation, output, and employment all fall

2. a. A positive IS curve shock which is temporary leads to rising interest rates, but no lasting effects on inflation and output
   b. A positive LM curve shock which is temporary leads to higher interest rates, inflation, and output
   c. A positive IS shock which is temporary leads to lower inflation, but to no changes in either interest rates or output
   d. A temporary revision of the expected rate of inflation downwards, leads to permanently lower interest rates and inflation but no permanent effect on any of the real variables

3. A neoclassical interpretation of the Great Depression includes:

   a. a cut in the growth rate of the money supply that shifted the LM curve to the left but did not lead to a change in inflation expectations
   b. a sharp rise in inflation expectations at the depth of the depression
   c. a loss of investor confidence which shifted the IS curve to the right
   d. shifts in the IS curve initially to the left and then to the right with no shift in the LM curve

4. The neoclassical decade (1958-1967) was a period in which:

   a. inflation expectations swung up and down
   b. the PA curve swung to and fro
   c. the IS curve swung to and fro
   d. both the PA and IS curves swung to and fro

5. a. The neoclassical model can explain fully the path of inflation since 1970
   b. The neoclassical model is unable to explain fully the co-movements of inflation and output in the 1970s
   c. The main shortcoming of the neoclassical model is its ability to predict the path of interest rates
   d. The neoclassical model would have predicted the 1970s very well if there had been no OPEC oil shock

6. The neoclassical model assumes that people are irrational because:

   a. they adjust their consumption demand all the time
   b. they create swings in the investment demand function
   c. they cannot work out how inflation is changing
   d. they do not adjust the expectation of inflation when they see inflation changing

7. a. The neoclassical model does not have a theory of how people formulate their expectations of inflation
   b. The neoclassical model lacks a good theory of how output and prices adjust to real world shocks
   c. If only the behavior of private agents was less volatile, then the neoclassical model would predict the business cycle very well
   d. Despite the differences between the neoclassical model and the basic model, neither of them is able to predict a positively sloped Phillips curve

True or False

1. The price adjustment curve in the neoclassical synthesis is a Phillips curve.

2. The neoclassical synthesis can predict both positive co-movements between inflation and output and also independent movements between them.

3. The neoclassical model predicts that the inflation rate will overshoot the money supply growth rate as they approach their new steady-state values.

4. The neoclassical model and the basic model predict very different things regarding the slope of the Phillips curve. The neoclassical model predicts a positively sloped Phillips curve whereas the basic model predicts a vertical Phillips curve.

5. The neoclassical model is unable to predict negative co-movements between inflation and output.

6. The only way the neoclassical model can be made to account for the facts of the 1970s is by supposing that there were sizable shifts in inflation expectations.

7. The Great Depression is accounted for by the neoclassical model as a result of two simultaneous shocks--a drop in inflation expectations and a cut the growth rate of the money supply.

Fill in the Blanks

1. An IS curve shock predicts a jump in interest rates and inflation. The rise in the nominal interest rate is ____________ than that in the inflation rate. On impact there is a __________________ in unemployment. In the steady state, the real and nominal interest rates are ____________ but inflation and output are ________________________ .

2. A rise in the money supply in the neoclassical synthesis predicts an immediate ____________ in interest rates, a ____________ in inflation and a ____________ in employment. At the point of impact the economy goes into ____________ . Inflation ____________ its steady-state level.

3. A temporary negative aggregate supply shock produces a temporary ____________ in interest rates, a ____________ in inflation and ____________, but there are no lasting effects on ____________ variables.

4. The major strengths of the neoclassical synthesis are its ability to account for the facts when ____________ ____________ are constant and to provide a framework for analyzing the consequences of ____________ in ____________ ____________ .

5. The major shortcoming of the neoclassical synthesis is its failure to predict ____________, given ______________________. The neoclassical synthesis has no theory of how ____________ expectations are formed or changed.

6. A deeper inadequacy in the model arises from the appearance of ____________________ on the part of the suppliers of ____________ . The only way in which the neoclassical synthesis can get away from the ____________________ ____________________ of the basic model is as a result of supposing that ____________ are willing to be ______ their ______ of ____________ ____________. ____________ gains from trades of labor between ______ and ____________ are simply assumed not to happen. This seeming ________________ is of concern because it stands in conflict with the assumptions that we make concerning all other aspects of human behavior.

Answers

Multiple Choice: 1 d 2 a 3 b 4 c 5 b 6 d 7 b
True or False: 1 T 2 F 3 T 4 T 5 T 6 T 7 T
Fill in the Blanks:
1. less, fall, higher, at their initial levels
2. fall, rise, rise, boom, overshoots
3. rise, fall, output, all
4. inflation expectations, changes, inflation expectations
5. inflation, the level of excess demand, inflation
6. irrationality, labor, full-employment equilibrium, workers, "off", supply, labor curves, mutual, firms, households, irrationality

CHAPTER 23

INTRODUCTION TO RATIONAL EXPECTATIONS THEORIES OF INCOME, EMPLOYMENT AND THE PRICE LEVEL

This short chapter introduces the next part of the book--the rational expectation theories of income, employment and the price level. Before beginning this next part be sure that you are familiar with:

(i) The questions that macroeconomics seeks to answer.
(ii) U.S. economic history since 1900 and the way in which the main macro variables are measured in the United States.
(iii) The definition of the business cycle and the co-movements among the variables along the cycle.
(iv) How the basic model explains the main trends in inflation but predicts that movements in prices (and in inflation) will be independent of movements in real variables.
(v) How the Keynesian model accounts for the procyclical co-movements of prices, but not for some of the strong outbursts in inflation that have occurred in the last decade.

You are now about to begin a very exciting part of the book. This part introduces you to recent innovations in macroeconomic theory which seek to overcome the shortcomings of both the basic and the Keynesian models.

When you have completed your study of this chapter you will:

Know the main components of the rational expectations theories of income, employment, and the price level.

Chapter Summary

The rational expectations theories of income, employment, and the price level seek to explain the procyclical co-movements of prices and, at the same time, to account for the important independent movements that occasionally occur between output and prices. They achieve this by radically modifying the neoclassical theory of aggregate supply, although accepting the neoclassical theory of aggregate demand. The new theories of aggregate supply generalize that of the basic model by introducing the expectations-augmented aggregate supply curve. These theories also incorporate the notion of rational expectations which assumes that people form their expectations on the basis of all the information available to them. That is, they assume that people are rational, do not waste information, and behave in the most efficient and economical manner that they can.

CHAPTER 24

INFORMATION, EXPECTATIONS, AND THE NEW CLASSICAL THEORY OF AGGREGATE SUPPLY

When you have completed your study of this chapter you will:

(a) Understand how incomplete information affects the supply of and demand for labor.
(b) Understand how the money wage and level of employment (and unemployment) are affected by wrong expectations.
(c) Know the definition of the expectations-augmented aggregate supply curve.
(d) Know how to derive the expectations-augmented aggregate supply curve.

Chapter Summary

A. Incomplete Information and the Labor Market

Because it is costly for workers to find suitable jobs and because it is costly for firms to find suitable employees, individuals typically do not change their jobs frequently, and labor is not traded as if in a continuous auction market. Rather, contracts are entered into which run for a year or more. Because contracts last for a sizable length of time and because it is expensive to write complicated contracts with detailed contingency clauses, it is typically the case that firms and households fix the price at which they will buy and sell labor in money units--i.e., they fix the money wage. However, because their decisions to buy and sell labor are influenced by the real wage, it is necessary for both households and firms to form an expectation about the price level that will prevail over the wage contract period.

Firms and households can do a better job of forming a reliable expectation about the prices in their own sector of the economy than they can about prices in general. Firms typically sell a small number of commodities and have a large amount of information about the markets in which they operate. Households buy a very large range of commodities and are not typically well informed about prices in all those markets. As an approximation it is assumed everyone knows the prices at which they will be selling their own output over the wage contract period. No one knows <u>all</u> the prices which they will be facing when buying, so it is necessary to form an expectation of those prices based on incomplete information.

B. Wrong Expectations and the Labor Market

For a given expectation of prices, a rise in the money wage will be read by households as a rise in the real wage, and they will increase the supply of labor. A cut in the money wage will be read as a cut in the real wage, and they will decrease their supply of labor. However, each firm, knowing the prices of its own limited range of commodities, will not be misinformed about the real wage it is paying, and the demand for labor will depend on the <u>actual</u> real wage. The higher is the actual price level relative to the expected price level, the lower will be the real wage, the greater will be the amount of labor which firms will hire, the higher will be the expected real wage, and the greater will be the amount of labor which households supply. There are many equilibrium levels of the real wage and of employment. The only equilibrium that corresponds to that in the basic model is the one in which the expected price level is equal to the actual price level. This occurs when everyone's expectation is correct.

C. Definition of the Expectations-Augmented Aggregate Supply Curve

The expectations-augmented aggregate supply curve traces out the quantities of aggregate output which firms would be willing to supply as the price level varies, at a given expected price level.

D. Derivation of the Expectations-Augmented Aggregate Supply Curve

The expectations-augmented aggregate supply curve is derived in Figure 24.3 of the textbook (p. 361). You should review that figure until you are thoroughly familiar with the derivation of the expectations-augmented aggregate supply curve.

Multiple Choice

1. In the new classical labor market:

   a. firms have more information than do households about the prices of goods in their own sector
   b. both households and firms have to form an expectation of the price of the good that the firm is producing before the money wage contract can be signed
   c. each firm knows all the prices of the goods produced in the economy whereas each household knows only the prices of a few of these goods
   d. the information that households and firms have is not different. They both know the prices of goods in their own sector of the economy but not all the prices of goods in the other sectors

2. In the new classical labor market the agreed money wage depends:

   a. only on the actual price level
   b. only on households' expectation of the real wage
   c. on both the actual price level and the expectation of the price level
   d. on both the actual and the expected real wage

3. In the new classical labor market:

   a. if the expected price increases when the actual price does so too does the money wage
   b. if the actual price decreases the money wage falls but the level of employment is constant
   c. if both the actual and the expected price levels rise by the same percentage amount then the money wage rises by the same percentage amount but the level of employment could rise or fall
   d. if the expected price level rises by less than does the actual price level, the money wage rises by less than the expected price level and employment falls

4. In the new classical labor market:

   a. firms always maximize profits and households always maximize expected utility
   b. firms always maximize profits and households rarely maximize utility
   c. either firms maximize profits or households maximize utility but not both
   d. firms always maximize profits and households sometimes maximize expected utility

5. In the new classical labor market:

   a. if the expected price level is 10% higher than the actual price level then there is 10% unemployment
   b. employment rises if the actual real wage exceeds that expected
   c. if the expected real wage rises then the equilibrium level of employment exceeds full employment
   d. if the expected real wage exceeds the actual then the actual level of employment is greater than that expected

6. a. The EAS curve shows what the economy is able to produce given households' willingness to work at the contracted money wage
   b. Along the EAS curve households maximize utility and firms maximize profits
   c. As the expected price level rises output rises along the EAS curve
   d. If the expected price level rises, the EAS curve shifts such that the same level of output will only be produced at a higher price level

True or False

1. Households expect the market to clear at full employment.

2. If the level of employment is below full employment households' expectation of the price level was too low.

3. On the average, households' expectation of the price level is correct.

4. Changes in the expected real wage arise only because households revise their forecast of the price level. Changing labor market conditions do not influence the expected real wage.

5. The EAS and the AS curves intersect at the expected price level.

6. If the expected price level rises, the EAS curve shifts upwards, the AS curve remains steady and the demand for labor curve shifts upwards.

7. If the average price level expected by households is less than the actual price level, then households will not maximize utility but the labor market clears at over-full employment.

Fill in the Blanks

1. Labor market contracts fix the ____________ wage at which labor will be willingly supplied and hired. These contracts exist mainly because it is ____________ for firms to find employees and ____________ for households to find employment.

2. There is an ____________ in the labor market but it is not an ____________ of ____________________. Both households and firms have the ____________ information concerning their own sector. Firms sell goods in their own sector therefore they ____________ the price at which their output will sell. Households buy goods sold in ____________ sectors of the economy and ____________ the prices of all these goods. Households have to form an ____________ of these prices, based on ____________ information.

Problem

Consider an economy described by the following equations and where the labor market is new classical. The production function is

$$y^s = 20n - 0.1n^2$$

The demand for labor is

$$n^d = 100 - 5(W/P)$$

The supply of labor is

$$n^s = 5(W/P^e)$$

The labor force is

$$\ell f = 6(W/P^e)$$

Calculate at full employment:

(a) the level of employment
(b) the real wage
(c) the money wage when the price level is \$1
(d) the size of the labor force

If the expected price level is \$1.2, calculate:

(e) the money wage
(f) the level of employment
(g) the size of the labor force
(h) the level of output
(i) the real wage
(j) the expected real wage

If the expected price level is $0.8, calculate:

(k) the money wage
(ℓ) the level of employment
(m) the size of the labor force
(n) the level of output
(o) the real wage
(p) the expected real wage
(q) the expected employment level
(r) the expected unemployment level
(s) the actual unemployment level

Answers

Multiple Choice: 1 d 2 c 3 d 4 a 5 d 6 d
True or False: 1 T 2 T 3 T 4 F 5 T 6 F 7 T
Fill in the Blanks:
1. money, costly, costly
2. asymmetry, asymmetry, information, same, known, many, do not know, expectation, incomplete
Problem: (a) 50 (b) 10 (c) $10 (d) 60 (e) 10.9 (f) 45.5 (g) 54.5 (h) 702 (i) 10.9 (j) 9.1 (k) 8.9 (ℓ) 55.6 (m) 66.7 (n) 802.9 (o) 8.9 (p) 11.1 (q) 50 (r) the natural rate (s) 11.1

CHAPTER 25

THE NEW KEYNESIAN THEORY OF AGGREGATE SUPPLY

When you have completed your study of this chapter you will:

(a) Know the key assumptions of the new Keynesian analysis.
(b) Understand how money wages are determined in the new Keynesian theory of aggregate supply.
(c) Understand the implications of the new Keynesian theory of wage determination for the expectations-augmented aggregate supply curve.
(d) Understand the implications of overlapping labor market contracts.

Chapter Summary

A. Assumptions of the New Keynesian Analysis

There are four key assumptions of the new Keynesian analysis:

1. Money wages are set for an agreed period and do not continuously adjust.
2. The actual quantity of labor traded is determined by the quantity demanded.
3. Money wages are set so as to achieve equality between the expected supply and expected demand for labor.
4. Wage contracts last for a longer term than the frequency with which the economy is hit by shocks and overlap in time.

B. Determination of Money Wages

Money wages are determined in the new Keynesian theory of aggregate supply by equating the supply of labor that is expected on the basis of the expected price level with the demand for labor that is expected on the basis of the expected price level. Figure 25.1 (p. 369 of the textbook) illustrates this relationship and should be thoroughly understood.

C. The New Keynesian Expectations-Augmented Aggregate Supply Curve

The new Keynesian theory of wage determination implies that the expectations-augmented aggregate supply curve will have the same basic shape as the new classical expectations-augmented aggregate supply curve. The new Keynesian aggregate supply curve will, however, be flatter than the new classical curve. This arises because, when the demand for labor function shifts because of changes in the actual price level, there are no partially compensating adjustments in the money wage to dampen off some of the effects of the shift in the demand curve on the quantity demanded. The quantity of labor demanded adjusts fully to reflect shifts in the demand function at the fixed money wage rate, and the level of output therefore fluctuates by a larger amount than otherwise would be the case.

D. Overlapping Wage Contracts

The fact that not all labor market contracts are signed on the same date, but overlap each other, has fundamental implications for the aggregate supply curve. Instead of the position of the aggregate supply curve depending only upon current expectations of the price level, it will also depend upon previous expectations of the current period's price level. Expectations formed in the past and now known to be wrong will be embodied in the position of the Keynesian expectations-augmented aggregate supply curve.

Multiple Choice

1. In the new Keynesian labor market:

   a. the level of employment depends upon the expected price level
   b. as the expected price level rises, the contracted money wage rises by the same percentage amount
   c. when the level of employment is below full employment the real wage expected by households must have been less than that expected by firms
   d. the money wage contracted can rise but never fall

2. In the new Keynesian labor market:

   a. the money wage depends upon the expected price level whereas the employment level depends upon the actual price level
   b. once the wage contract is signed the number of people employed is determined by the supply of labor
   c. firms always maximize profits as they do a better job at forecasting the price level than do households
   d. if the demand for labor was perfectly elastic, households would play no role in the determination of the money wage or the level of employment

3. The new Keynesian aggregate supply curve:

   a. is the same as the new classical aggregate supply curve
   b. is steeper than the new classical aggregate supply curve and they intersect on the basic model's aggregate supply curve
   c. is flatter than the new classical aggregate supply curve and they intersect at the expected price level
   d. cannot be compared with the new classical aggregate supply curve because the contracted wage in the two labor markets under identical conditions would be different

4. The new Keynesian labor market:

   a. is really the same as the Keynesian labor market--the money wage is rigid
   b. generates an AS curve which is the same as the Keynesian AS curve
   c. incorporates inflexibility in the money wage because wage contracts are overlapping. This inflexibility is similar to the rigidity in the money wage in the Keynesian model
   d. does not resemble the Keynesian labor market at all, as it does not assume wage contracts of any kind (overlapping or not)

5. If the expected price level is greater than the actual:

   a. there is less unemployment in the new Keynesian than in the new classical model
   b. the expected real wage is higher in the new classical than in the new Keynesian model
   c. the money wage in the new Keynesian is higher than that in the new classical model
   d. the expected employment level is lower in the new classical than in the new Keynesian model

True or False

1. The new Keynesian EAS curve is always flatter than the new classical EAS curve.

2. Once the wage contract is signed the supply of labor becomes horizontal.

3. If the expected price level is incorrect households do not maximize utility and firms do not maximize profits.

4. If the expected price level turns out to be too high then the actual real wage exceeds that which was expected and the level of employment also exceeds that which was expected.

5. Because contracts are overlapping money wages are autocorrelated. This is the new way of rationalizing the Keynesian assumption of "sticky money wages".

Fill in the Blanks

1. The four assumptions of the new Keynesian analysis are: (i) ____________ wages are set for an agreed ____________ and do not ____________ adjust; (ii) the actual quantity of labor traded is determined by the quantity ____________; (iii) ____________ wages are set so as to achieve ____________ between ____________ supply and ____________ demand for labor; and (iv) wage contracts last for a ____________ term than the frequency with which the economy is hit by ____________ and ____________ in time.

2. ____________ wages are determined by equating the ____________ supply of labor with the ____________ demand for labor.

3. The new Keynesian aggregate supply curve will be ____________ than the new classical curve because, when the actual price level changes, there are no ____________ ____________ ____________ in the money wage to dampen off some of the effects of the shift in the ____________ curve on the quantity demanded.

4. Because not all labor contracts are signed on the same date the position of the aggregate supply curve depends not only on ____________ expectations of the price level but also on ____________ expectations of the current period's price level. Expectations formed all the way back to the date on which the ____________ existing contract was signed will be ____________ in the position of the Keynesian expectations-augmented aggregate supply curve.

Problems

Rework the Problems 1 and 2 of the previous chapter, assuming now that the labor market is characterized by the new Keynesian model rather than the new classical.

Answers

Multiple Choice: 1 b 2 a 3 c 4 c 5 c
True or False: 1 T 2 T 3 F 4 F 5 T
Fill in the Blanks:
1. money, period, continuously, demanded, money, equality, expected, expected, longer, shocks, overlap
2. money, expected, expected
3. flatter, partially compensating adjustments, demand
4. current, previous, oldest, embodied

Problems: 1. (a) 50 (b) 10 (c) \$10 (d) 60 (e) \$12 (f) 40 (g) 60 (h) 640 (i) 12 (j) 10

2. (a) $y = 750$ (b) $y = 1000 - 360/P^2$

CHAPTER 26

EQUILIBRIUM INCOME, EMPLOYMENT, AND THE PRICE LEVEL WITH FIXED EXPECTATIONS

When you have completed your study of this chapter you will:

(a) Know the definition of full-employment equilibrium.
(b) Know how to characterize full-employment equilibrium in a simple diagram.
(c) Understand how output, employment, the real wage, the price level, and the money wage are affected by a rise or fall in aggregate demand when the expected price level is fixed.
(d) Understand how output, employment, the real wage, the price level, and the money wage are affected by a rise or fall in the expected price level when aggregate demand is fixed.

Chapter Summary

A. Full-Employment Equilibrium

Full-employment equilibrium values of output, employment, unemployment, and the real wage occur when the actual price level is equal to the expected price level. The unemployment present at full-employment equilibrium is called the natural rate of unemployment.

B. Simple Diagram to Characterize Full-Employment Equilibrium

Figure 26.1 of the textbook (p. 378) is a diagram of full-employment equilibrium, and you should be thoroughly familiar with it. You should also understand that it is identical to the equilibrium in the basic model which was examined in Chapter 10 of the textbook (pp. 137-43).

C. Effects of Change in Aggregate Demand with a Fixed Price Level

If the expected price level is fixed, a rise in aggregate demand will raise the level of output, employment, and the price level. It will lower the real wage and will make unemployment fall below its natural rate.

When the expected price level is fixed and aggregate demand falls, there will be a fall in output, employment, and in the price level. The real wage will rise, and unemployment will rise above its natural rate.

D. Effects of a Change in the Expected Price Level with Constant Aggregate Demand

If aggregate demand is fixed, a rise in the expected price level will raise the actual price level but by less than the expected price level has increased, and it will lower output. Real wages and unemployment will rise, and employment will fall. Money wages will rise by more than the price level but by less than the expected price level. When aggregate demand is fixed and the expected price level falls, the actual price level will fall, and output will rise. The fall in the actual price level will be less than the fall in the expected price level. Real wages will fall, but expected real wages will rise. Unemployment will also fall below its natural rate.

Multiple Choice

1. a. There is no unemployment at the full-employment equilibrium
   b. Full-employment equilibrium occurs when the expectation of the price level turns out to be correct
   c. The natural rate of unemployment is a constant which naturally occurs in the labor market
   d. The full-employment equilibrium is defined as the equilibrium when there is no unemployment in the labor market

2. If the expected price level is fixed and the actual price level rises:

   a. the natural rate of unemployment falls
   b. the economy experiences a boom with unemployment falling
   c. employment rises and this shifts the AS curve to the right
   d. aggregate demand shifts to the left and this reduces the expansionary effect on the economy

3. If the expected price level is fixed and aggregate demand rises:

   a. the price level rises
   b. the real wage rises
   c. employment falls
   d. output falls

4. If the expected price level is constant and aggregate demand falls:

   a. the economy moves down the AS curve
   b. the level of output falls along the EAS curve
   c. the real wage falls
   d. forces in the economy will cause the level of aggregate demand to return to its initial level

5. A 5% fall in the expected price level when aggregate demand is constant lowers:

   a. output by 5%
   b. the price level by 5%
   c. the price level by less than 5%
   d. the real wage by 5%

6. A 10% rise in the expected price level and a 10% rise in aggregate demand will:

   a. not affect the actual price level
   b. raise unemployment by 10%
   c. raise the money wage by 10%
   d. raise aggregate supply by 10%

True or False

1. In a new Keynesian model, if the expected price level falls and if the money supply remains constant, real income rises and the expected real wage rises.

2. In a new classical model, if the expected price level falls but the money supply remains constant, real wages rise, the level of employment falls and the price level rises.

3. In a new classical model, if the expected price level is constant but aggregate demand rises by 10%, then the actual price level and output both rise but each of them rises by less than 10%.

4. In a new classical model, if the expected price level and the level of aggregate demand each fall by 10% then money wages fall by 10% and the expected real wage also falls by 10%.

5. In a new Keynesian model if the expected price level and the level of aggregate demand each fall by 10%, then the level of output rises, the level of employment rises, and real wages fall.

6. If the expected price level falls by 10% but aggregate demand rises by 10% the price level may rise or fall but output rises, the expected real wage rises, but the actual real wage falls.

Fill in the Blanks

1. The level of unemployment at the full-employment equilibrium is called the ___________ rate of unemployment. The level of unemployment can exceed (or fall short) of the natural rate of unemployment depending upon whether the ___________ price level exceeds (or falls short) of the ___________ price level.

2. If the expected price level is fixed and aggregate demand rises then the level of output ___________, employment ___________, and the price level ___________. It will ___________ the real wage and will make unemployment ___________ its natural rate.

3. When the expected price level is fixed and aggregate demand falls, there will be a ___________ in output, employment, and in the price level. The real wage will ___________, and unemployment will ___________ its natural rate.

4. When the expected price level is fixed and aggregate demand rises the economy will move ______ the EAS curve to a ___________ price level and ___________ output level.

5. If aggregate demand is constant and the expected price level falls there will be a ____________ in the price level, a ____________ in output, a ____________ in the real wage, and a ____________ in the expected real wage.

Problem

Consider an economy in which the production function is

$$y = 240n - 0.5n^2$$

The labor demand curve is

$$n^d = 240 - W/P^e$$

The labor supply curve is

$$n^s = W/P^e$$

Aggregate demand is

$$y^d = M/P$$

Calculate:

(a) the full-employment level of employment
(b) the full-employment level of output

If the expected price level is \$0.5 and the money stock is \$10,800 calculate:

(c) the level of employment
(d) the money wage
(e) the real wage
(f) the expected real wage
(g) the expected level of employment

If the expected price level remains at \$0.5 but the money stock falls to \$9,000 calculate:

(h) the level of output
(i) the price level

Answers

Multiple Choice: 1 b 2 b 3 a 4 b 5 c 6 c
True or False: 1 T 2 F 3 T 4 F 5 F 6 T
Fill in the Blanks:
1. natural, expected, actual
2. rises, rises, rises, lower, fall below
3. fall, rise, exceed
4. up, higher, higher
5. fall, rise, fall, rise
Problem:
(a) 120 (b) 21,600 (c) 21,600 (d) 60 (e) 120 (f) 120 (g) 120
(h) 19911.1 (i) 0.45

CHAPTER 27

PRICE LEVEL EXPECTATIONS

When you have completed your study of this chapter you will:

(a) Understand the relationship between the expected price level and the expected rate of inflation.
(b) Understand the distinction between a subjective expectation and a conditional mathematical expectation.
(c) Understand why wrong expectations are costly.
(d) Understand the concept of a rational expectation.
(e) Understand the concept of the rational expectation of the price level.
(f) Know how to work out the rational expectation of the price level.

Chapter Summary

A. The Expected Price Level and the Expected Rate of Inflation

The expected rate of inflation is equal to the expected price level minus the previous price level expressed as a percentage of the previous price level. It is not the percentage change in the expected price level but rather the expected change in the price level.

B. The Distinction Between a Subjective Expectation and a Conditional Mathematical Expectation

A subjective expectation is a vague intuitive feeling about the likely value or outcome of some future event. A conditional mathematical expectation is the true average value of the outcome of a future event conditional on (i.e., given) whatever are the known actual values of all the relevant variables.

C. Why Wrong Expectations Are Costly

Actions are based on expectations, and wrong expectations lead to actions that may turn out to be inappropriate. If the price turns out to be higher than was expected, real wages will turn out to be lower than was expected, and people will end up doing more work and consuming less leisure than they would have liked to have done had they known the correct real wage rate ahead of time. A symmetric cost applies to an error in the opposite direction. It is important to distinguish between being right every time (which in general is impossible) and being right on the average. The casino example in the text (p. 395) illustrates this distinction.

D. Rational Expectation

A rational expectation of a variable is a subjective expectation which coincides with the conditional mathematical expectation of that variable, given the available information.

E. Rational Expectation of the Price Level

The rational expectation of the price level is the prediction of the price level that is based on all the available information at the time at which the expectation is formed. That information includes the body of economic theory relevant for predicting a price level.

F. How to Work Out the Rational Expectation of the Price Level

The rational expectation of the price level in the context of the new theories is the price level at which the expected aggregate demand curve cuts the aggregate supply curve. (The conceptual experiment whereby this expectation is worked out is discussed in the section on rational expectation and illustrated in Figure 27.2 on page 402 of the textbook and should be thoroughly understood.)

Multiple Choice

1. If the price level in year 0 is 90 and the expectation is that the price level in year 1 will be 95, then the expected inflation rate is:

   a. 5
   b. $0.0\dot{5}$
   c. $5.\dot{5}\%$
   d. 5.26%

2. A rational expectation is:

   a. a wild guess
   b. a subjective expectation based on an educated guess
   c. a conditional mathematical expectation given all the available information
   d. a subjective expectation that coincides with the conditional mathematical expectation given all the available information

3. a. A subjective expectation is a guess
   b. A mathematical expectation is an average
   c. A forecast given by an expert is always a rational expectation
   d. A mathematical expectation is an intuitive feeling

4. The rational expectation of the price level is determined by:

   a. full-employment output and a vague feeling of what will happen in the next period
   b. full-employment output and expected aggregate demand
   c. the expectations-augmented aggregate supply curve and expected aggregate demand
   d. actual aggregate demand and the money wage contracted

5. A rational expectation of the price level is:

   a. a forecast based on all available information
   b. a subjective forecast
   c. a guess
   d. a forecast that is correct

6. a. The higher is the expected money supply, the higher is the rational expectation of the price level
   b. If the expectation is that there will be a balanced budget rise in government expenditure, the rational expectation of the price level does not rise
   c. If the expectation is that fiscal policy will be contracted, then the rational expectation of the price level does not change
   d. If the expected price level rises, then it is rational for the government to raise the money supply so as to match the expected rise in the price level

True or False

1. If the price level is expected to rise, then expected inflation rises.

2. If the expectation is that the money supply will rise so that expected aggregate demand rises by 10%, then the rational expectation of the price level is that it will also rise by 10%.

3. If an expectation of the price level predicts an actual price level that does not equal that expected, then the expectation is not rational.

4. The rational expectation of the price level may be greater than, equal to, or less than the actual price level.

5. The term rational expectation is just a fancy name for perfect foresight.

6. The rational expectation of the price level rises if the expectations-augmented aggregate supply curve shifts upwards.

Fill in the Blanks

1. The expected rate of inflation is equal to the ___________ price level minus the ___________ price level expressed as a ___________ of the ___________ price level.

2. A subjective expectation is a vague ___________ ___________ about the likely outcome of some future event.

3. A conditional mathematical expectation is the value of the outcome of a future event conditional on all ___________ ___________ values of the ___________ variables.

4. A rational expectation of a variable is a ______________________ expectation which ___________ with the conditional mathematical expectation of that variable, ______________________________________.

5. In forming a rational expectation of the price level, all the available information includes the body of ___________ ___________ relevant for predicting the price level.

6. An expectation of the price level is rational if the actual price level ___________ by the relevant economic theory equals that ___________ ___________ ___________.

Problem

Consider an economy in which the production function is

$$y = 240n - 0.5n^2$$

The labor demand curve is

$$n^d = 240 - W/P^e$$

The labor supply is

$$n^s = W/P^e$$

Aggregate demand is

$$y^d = M/P$$

(a) Calculate the rational expectation of the price level if the expected money supply is \$25,920.
(b) If the expected money supply rises by 10%, by how much does the expected price level rise?
(c) If the labor market was new classical rather than new Keynesian, what now is your answer to (a) above?

Answers

Multiple Choice: 1 c 2 d 3 b 4 b 5 a 6 a
True or False: 1 F 2 T 3 T 4 T 5 F 6 F
Fill in the Blanks:
1. expected, previous, percentage, previous
2. intuitive feeling
3. known actual, relevant
4. subjective, coincides, given all the available information
5. economic theory
6. predicted, expected price level
Problem: (a) \$1.20 (b) 10% (c) \$1.20

CHAPTER 28

EQUILIBRIUM INCOME, EMPLOYMENT, AND THE PRICE LEVEL WITH RATIONAL EXPECTATIONS

When you have completed your study of this chapter you will:

(a) Understand the distinction between an anticipated and unanticipated change in aggregate demand.
(b) Know how output, employment, unemployment, the real wage, money wage, and price level are affected by an anticipated change in aggregate demand.
(c) Know how output, employment, unemployment, the real wage, money wage, and price level are affected by an unanticipated change in aggregate demand.

Chapter Summary

A. Anticipated and Unanticipated Change in Aggregate Demand

The change in aggregate demand may be decomposed into its anticipated or expected component and its unanticipated or unexpected component. The anticipated change in aggregate demand may be greater or smaller than the actual change. When the anticipated change is exactly the same as the actual change we speak of a fully anticipated change in aggregate demand. The unanticipated change in aggregate demand is simply the difference between the actual and the anticipated changes. Since the change in actual aggregate demand is determined by changes in the money supply, government spending, and taxes, decomposing the change in aggregate demand into its expected and unexpected components involves decomposing the changes in these determinants of aggregate demand into their anticipated and unanticipated components.

B. Effects of an Anticipated Change in Aggregate Demand

An anticipated change in aggregate demand has the effect of changing the price level and the money wage by exactly the same percentage amount as each other and by the same percentage amount as the rise in aggregate demand. It has no effects on any of the real variables. Specifically, it has no effect on output, employment, unemployment, or the real wage.

C. Effects of an Unanticipated Change in Aggregate Demand

An unanticipated change in aggregate demand has both real and nominal effects. It will raise the price level, but by a smaller percentage amount than the unanticipated rise in aggregate demand, and it will raise the money wage rate by an even smaller percentage amount than it raises the price level. It thus will lower the real wage, raise the level of employment, raise the level of output, and lower the level of unemployment.

Multiple Choice

1. A 10% unanticipated cut in the money stock:

   a. lowers the price level by 10%
   b. lowers the money wage by more than the drop in the price level
   c. lowers the expected real wage by less than 10%
   d. lowers the actual real wage by less than 10%

2. An anticipated fall in the money stock:

   a. lowers the price level and raises the actual real wage
   b. lowers the money wage
   c. lowers the expected real wage
   d. lowers the level of employment

3. An expected cut in the money supply that exceeds an actual cut in the money supply will:

   a. leave the price level unchanged
   b. lower the money wage but raise the real wage
   c. lower the level of employment
   d. lower the expected real wage

4. A rise in the money supply that exceeds that expected will:

   a. raise output and raise employment
   b. raise the price level but lower the money wage
   c. raise the real wage
   d. lower the expected real wage

5. An anticipated rise in the money stock:

   a. raises output
   b. lowers the real wage
   c. raises the price level but by more than the rise in the money wage
   d. makes no change in the actual real wage

True or False

1. If the economy is initially in steady-state equilibrium with output growing at 3% per annum and the money supply growing at 10% per annum, then the steady-state inflation rate is 7% per annum. If the money stock is expected to grow in the future at 15% per annum but in fact only grows at 12% per annum the inflation rate rises to something between 9% and 12% and output falls below full employment.

2. An unanticipated cut in the money supply will have bigger price level effects and lower output effects if the labor market is new Keynesian rather than new classical.

3. An unanticipated rise in aggregate demand of 10% will cause the price level to rise by 5% and output to rise also by 5%.

4. An anticipated rise in government expenditure which raises the aggregate demand curve by 10% will cause the expected price level and the actual price level to rise initially by more than 10%.

5. A permanent tax cut not matched by a cut in government spending will raise the rate of inflation.

Fill in the Blanks

1. The unanticipated change in aggregate demand equals the ___________ change in aggregate demand less the _______________ change in aggregate demand.

2. An anticipated rise in aggregate demand raises the ___________ and the ___________ but does not change the levels of ___________, ___________, ___________, and the ___________.

3. An unanticipated fall in aggregate demand lowers the ___________, ___________, and __________ and raises the ___________, and ___________.

4. If the expectation is that aggregate demand will fall when in fact it rises, then the price level ___________ and output ___________. The real wage ___________ and unemployment ___________.

5. A 10% rise in expected aggregate demand when the actual level of aggregate demand rises 7% leads to a _____% rise in the expected price level, a _____% rise in the actual price level and a rise in output equal to _________________________.

Problem

Consider an economy in which aggregate supply is

$$y^* = 750$$

Aggregate demand is

$$y^d = M/P$$

The expectations-augmented aggregate supply is

$$y^s = (1000P^2 - 250(P^e)^2)/P^2$$

If the expected money supply is \$1500, calculate:

(a) the rational expectation of the price level
(b) the expected output level

If the actual money supply is $1600, calculate:

(c) the actual price level
(d) the actual output level

If the labor market is new Keynesian and the expected real wage is 10, calculate:

(e) the actual real wage

Answers

Multiple Choice: 1 c 2 b 3 d 4 a 5 d
True or False: 1 T 2 F 3 F 4 T 5 T
Fill in the Blanks:
1. actual, anticipated
2. price level, money wage, output, employment, unemployment, real wage
3. price level, output, employment, real wage, unemployment
4. rises, rises, falls, falls
5. 10, < 7, 10% minus the percentage rise in the price level
Problem: (a) $2 (b) 750 (c) $2.08 (d) 769.0 (e) 9.6

CHAPTER 29

EXPLAINING THE FACTS

When you have completed your study of this chapter you will:

(a) Understand how unanticipated changes in aggregate demand generate procyclical co-movements in prices.
(b) Understand how a combination of unanticipated and anticipated changes in aggregate demand generates surges in inflation which are independent of output, and also generates procyclical co-movements in prices.
(c) Know how the rational expectations theories explain the autocorrelation of output and employment.
(d) Understand the implications of rational expectations for interest rate behavior.
(e) Understand how rational expectations theories explain the business cycle.
(f) Understand the nature of the hypothesis testing problem posed by the rational expectations theories.

Chapter Summary

A. Procyclical Co-Movements in Prices

Generally, the swings in the actual values of variables that determine aggregate demand (for example, the money supply) are bigger than the swings in the anticipated values of those variables. This means that the aggregate demand curve fluctuates with greater amplitude than the expectations-augmented aggregate supply curve. The consequence of this is procyclical co-movements of prices in general.

B. Independent Movements in Output and Prices

Anticipated changes in aggregate demand will move the price level but leave output undisturbed, whereas unanticipated changes in aggregate demand will move the price level and output. By combining anticipated and unanticipated movements in aggregate demand (generated by anticipated and unanticipated movements in monetary and fiscal policy variables) we are able, in principle, to account for the facts about output and prices (or, equivalently, unemployment and inflation). As a general rule, prices are procyclical (inflation and unemployment are negatively related) for the reasons summarized above. Occasionally there will be a surge in inflation that is independent of, or even sometimes goes in the same direction as, the unemployment rate. This will arise because the anticipated rise in the money supply is high, whereas the unanticipated change in the money supply is negative.

C. Autocorrelation of Output and Employment

Output is autocorrelated even though the shocks that hit the economy are purely random because the costs of changing labor inputs and overlapping labor contracts impart inertia into firms' adjustments of employment and output.

D. Interest Rate Behavior

Money rates of interest will exceed real rates of interest by an amount equal to the anticipated rate of inflation. The term over which inflation has to be anticipated is the same as the term over which a loan is made. For three-month loans, the relevant anticipated inflation rate is that over the next three months. For twenty-year loans, the average anticipation of average inflation over the next twenty years is required. Anticipated inflation depends only on anticipated money growth, whereas actual inflation depends on both anticipated and unanticipated money growth. Interest rates will fluctuate in a generally procyclical manner but with less amplitude than prices because the anticipated money supply growth rate will fluctuate with a smaller amplitude than the actual money supply growth rate. Longer-term interest rates will have an even smaller amplitude of fluctuation because fluctuations in the anticipated long-term average money supply growth rate will have smaller amplitude than those of short-term anticipations.

E. The Business Cycle

The first feature of the business cycle, the autocorrelation of output, is explained by the costs of adjusting labor inputs and overlapping labor market contracts. The procyclical co-movements of prices and interest rates are explained by the tendency for the actual variables that generate aggregate demand (monetary and fiscal policy variables) to fluctuate with greater amplitude than their expected values. The nonuniversality of the procyclical co-movements of prices arises from the occasional jump in the anticipated money supply growth rate (sometimes in excess of that which actually occurs).

F. The Hypothesis Testing Problem Posed by Rational Expectations Theories

The major problem is that of finding a convincing and noncontroversial way of decomposing changes in the actual value of exogenous variables into their anticipated and unanticipated components. Discriminating between the new Keynesian and new classical theories will be difficult because they are almost equivalent from the observational point of view. Further, discriminating rational expectations theories from traditional theory purely on the basis of the past will be difficult since it is always possible to patch up the traditional theory with an appropriately general theory of time lags involved in the adjustment of expectations for the two theories to yield identical predictions. The ultimate test of any theory will lie in its ability to predict the future rather than the past.

Multiple Choice

1. Expected aggregate demand is:

   a. the highest level of aggregate demand in the past
   b. the lowest level of aggregate demand in the past
   c. the average level of aggregate demand in the past
   d. halfway between the highest and lowest levels of aggregate demand in the past

2. Actual aggregate demand:

a. fluctuates less than expected aggregate demand
b. is nearly always greater than or less than expected aggregate demand because random shocks can be either positive or negative
c. fluctuates about expected aggregate demand but on the average they are the same
d. really equals expected aggregate demand

3. An actual change in aggregate demand of:

a. 200 of which 100 was anticipated is an unanticipated change in aggregate demand of -100
b. -200 of which 100 was anticipated is an unanticipated change in aggregate demand of -100
c. -200 of which -100 was anticipated is an unanticipated change in aggregate demand of 100
d. -200 of which 100 was anticipated is an unanticipated change in aggregate demand of -300

4. An unanticipated rise in aggregate demand leads to:

a. a rise in both the price level and output
b. a rise in the price level but no change in output
c. a rise in output but a fall in the price level
d. a fall in both output and the price level

5. An anticipated rise in aggregate demand leads to:

a. a rise in the price level and in interest rates
b. a rise in output but interest rates may rise or fall
c. a change in output but interest rates may change or may not change
d. a fall in interest rates and no change in output

6. Random aggregate demand shocks to the economy:

a. lead to random movements in output
b. lead to output being autocorrelated because of inertia
c. lead to random fluctuations in prices but because of inertia output and unemployment are autocorrelated
d. are unanticipated, so output cannot be autocorrelated

True or False

1. An unanticipated rise in the money supply raises the price level, interest rates and output.

2. An anticipated tax cut of 100 financed by money printing raises the price level by more than an anticipated balanced budget cut of 100.

3. Random shocks to aggregate demand lead to procyclical co-movements in prices.

4. Anticipated changes in fiscal policy have the same effects on the price level in the rational expectations model as in the basic model.

5. Because random shocks are always hitting the economy there can be no independent movements of the price level and output.

Fill in the Blanks

1. The difference between the __________ change in aggregate demand and the anticipated change in aggregate demand is the change in aggregate demand that was __________ .

2. A constant expected growth rate of the money supply leads to a constant rate of __________ that __________ the rate of growth of the money supply.

3. __________ fluctuations in the growth rate of the money supply lead to __________ co-movements of prices.

4. Rational expectations theories are capable of accounting for procyclical, countercyclical and independent co-movements in __________ . __________ changes in aggregate demand lead to these __________ co-movements; __________ changes in aggregate demand lead to independent co-movements; and an __________ change (say rise) in aggregate demand that, in absolute terms, __________ the actual change (________) in aggregate demand leads to countercyclical co-movements.

5. Autocorrelation of output arises because of __________ ______ __________ in the new classical model and __________________ contracts in the new Keynesian model.

Answers

Multiple Choice: 1 c 2 c 3 d 4 a 5 c 6 b
True or False: 1 F 2 T 3 T 4 F 5 F
Fill in the Blanks:
1. actual, unanticipated
2. inflation, equals
3. random, procyclical
4. prices, unanticipated, procyclical, anticipated, expected, exceeds, fall
5. costs of adjustment, overlapping

CHAPTER 30

INTRODUCTION TO MACROECONOMIC POLICY PROBLEMS

This chapter introduces the next part of the book--macroeconomic policy. Before beginning to study this part, you should be sure that you are thoroughly familiar with:

- (i) The questions that macroeconomics seeks to answer.
- (ii) The economic history of the United States since 1900 and the way in which the main macro variables are measured in the United States.
- (iii) The definition of the business cycle and the co-movements among the variables along the cycle.
- (iv) How the basic model explains the main trends in inflation but predicts that movements in prices (and in inflation) will be independent of movements in the real variables.
- (v) How the Keynesian model accounts for the procyclical co-movements of prices, but not for some of the strong outbursts in inflation that have occurred in the last decade.
- (vi) How the rational expectations theories account for both the co-movements and independent movements of prices along the business cycle.

This part of the textbook examines the implications of the rational expectations theories for the formation and conduct of macroeconomic policy.

When you have completed your study of this chapter you will:

- (a) Know what macroeconomic policies seek to achieve.
- (b) Know the highlights in the evolution of the policy debate.
- (c) Understand the idea that policy is a process and not an event.

Chapter Summary

A. What Macroeconomic Policies Seek to Achieve

Macroeconomic policies seek to minimize fluctuations in unemployment and output about their natural rates and to minimize the variability of inflation around some low, stable, possibly zero, value. Other objectives, such as lowering the natural rate of unemployment, are not, strictly speaking, <u>macroeconomic</u> policies. They involve <u>microeconomic</u> intervention to change relative prices.

B. Highlights of the Evolution of Policy Debate

The pre-Keynesian view of macroeconomic policy was that nothing could be done. Fluctuations simply had to be lived with in the same way as other natural disorders. The Keynesian revolution led to the optimistic view that by manipulating monetary and fiscal policy, aggregate demand could be controlled in such a way as to achieve full employment and price stability. The new view is that because expectations are formed rationally, the best that policy can do is to avoid injecting uncertainty into the economy. Fully predictable policy is therefore required. It may be possible to achieve the best outcome with a pre-announced policy feedback rule, but it will not be possible to do better with <u>ad hoc</u> discretionary intervention.

C. The Idea that Policy is a Process and not an Event

If expectations are formed rationally, analyzing the implications of a policy change requires that it be decomposed into an anticipated and unanticipated component. Only by analyzing the entire process of policy is it possible to say whether a particular event was anticipated or unanticipated.

Multiple Choice

1. Ideal macroeconomic policy seeks to:

   a. reduce unemployment and inflation to zero
   b. lower interest rates so that home buyers face a fair interest rate
   c. keep inflation at a constant, steady, and low rate while reducing unemployment to the natural rate
   d. provide a job for every American who needs a job and at a fair wage

2. a. Classical economists conducted macroeconomic policy so that they could control the business cycle
   b. Keynesian macroeconomic policy was concerned with reducing unemployment to zero
   c. Keynesian economists believed they could control the business cycle whereas classical economists believed that they simply had to put up with the business cycle
   d. Rational expectations theories include random shocks. These shocks are uncontrollable and as a result economists believe that there is no possible way of controlling or manipulating the business cycle

3. Macroeconomic policy is:

   a. a single event
   b. not an event but a process
   c. both an event and a process and economic agents ought to try to understand both
   d. neither an event nor a process--it is purely the choice of the government

True or False

1. Rational expectations theories are based on the fact that as people become rational the business cycle will disappear.

2. Macroeconomic policy in the light of rational expectation theories must be analyzed as a process and not as an event.

3. Rational expectations theories lead to a radically different view of economic policy.

4. If only more people were rational, the rational expectations theories would lead to better policy.

5. Rational expectations theories assume perfect foresight.

Fill in the Blanks

1. The old fashioned way of looking at macroeconomic policy was to treat policy as an ____________ .

2. The new approach to policy is to treat policy as a ____________ so that the ____________ process is analyzed in order that a particular policy ____________ may be identified as anticipated, ____________ or partly one and partly the other.

3. Macroeconomic policy seeks to achieve ____________ unemployment, and ____________ , ____________ and ____________ inflation.

Answers

Multiple Choice: 1 c 2 c 3 b
True or False: 1 F 2 T 3 T 4 F 5 F
Fill in the Blanks:
1. event
2. process, entire, event, unanticipated
3. low, constant, steady, low

CHAPTER 31

THE CONSTRAINTS ON MONETARY AND FISCAL POLICY

When you have completed your study of this chapter you will:

(a) Understand the nature of the government budget constraint.
(b) Understand the implications of the government budget constraint for the conduct of monetary and fiscal policy.
(c) Understand the implications of the government budget constraint for the formation of rational expectations.

Chapter Summary

A. Government Budget Constraint

The government budget constraint states that total government expenditures on goods and services, transfers to individuals, and debt interest must equal receipts from legislative taxes, the sales of new debt, and the creation of new money.

B. Government Budget Constraint and the Conduct of Monetary and Fiscal Policy

Though the government can issue debt, thereby weakening the link between monetary and fiscal policy in the short run, on the average over the long term, debt interest has to be paid that exactly offsets the receipts from debt sales. This means that, in effect, issuing debt is the same thing as deferring taxes. The long-term average government budget constraint does not give the government the option of raising debt. There is, therefore, on the average, a fundamental connection between fiscal policy and monetary policy. Conventionally, legislative taxes together with the creation of new money must raise sufficient funds to cover the government's expenditure. Monetary policy and fiscal policy, on the average, are interdependent.

C. Government Budget Constraint and Formation of Rational Expectations

It will not be rational to form an expectation of long-term money growth and inflation that is based on a violation of the government's budget constraint. In a situation in which the government is currently running a deficit or surplus, and issuing (or retiring) large volumes of debt, individuals will have to form a rational expectation concerning which of the variables in the government's budget constraint will be varied in order to satisfy the long-term average budget constraint. In some situations it will be rational to expect a future burst of inflation, whereas in others it will be rational to expect continued mild inflation and adjustments of legislated taxes or expenditure.

Multiple Choice

1. a. Government payments include its expenditure on goods and services, transfer payments, debt interest payments and the net issue of currency
   b. Government receipts include legislated taxes, net issue of debt and debt interest
   c. Debt interest is a payment by the government and sales of debt are a government receipt
   d. Net issue of currency is neither a payment nor a receipt; it is merely the means of finalizing a purchase

2. a. The profit of the Fed is the net issue of new bank notes
   b. The change in the Fed's assets minus liabilities is the profit made by the Fed
   c. If the Fed's profit is determined by its assets and liabilities then it is always zero as its assets and liabilities always balance
   d. Since the Fed prints bank notes in order to buy government securities, its profit must be the sum of the net issue of new bank notes and the interest earned on its holdings of government securities

3. The government budget constraint in the short term is:

   a. $G + DI - NET\ TAX - \Delta D = 0$
   b. $G - NET\ TAX = 0$
   c. $G - NET\ TAX - \Delta MB = 0$
   d. $G + DI - NET\ TAX - \Delta D - \Delta MB = 0$

4. The government sells a bond that promises to pay $5 forever. The market rate of interest is 10%.

   a. If the price of the bond was $80 you would want to buy the bond
   b. If the price of the bond was $70 you would want to buy the bond
   c. If the price of the bond was $40 you would want to buy the bond
   d. The equilibrium price of the bond is $45

5. The government's fundamental budget constraint is:

   a. $G - T^* = \Delta MB$
   b. $g - t^*$ = the inflation tax
   c. $g - t^* = 0$
   d. $g - t^*$ = profit of the Fed

True or False

1. The government must balance its budget in the long run but in the short run it can run either a budget deficit or surplus.

2. The government can always finance its purchases of goods and services by selling bonds, even in the long run.

3. The government finances its purchases of goods and services by using whatever amount of inflation tax it chooses.

4. The government's budget constraint links fiscal and monetary policy so that they are not independent. This limits the ability of the government to use the inflation tax to cover its spending.

5. The government can finance its purchases of goods and services by legislated taxes, by selling bonds or by printing money. In the long run, however, it can cover its spending only by legislated taxes and the inflation tax.

Fill in the Blanks:

1. The government's payments are (i) ____________________,
(ii) ____________________, and (iii) ____________________.

2. The government's receipts are (i) ____________________,
(ii) ____________________, and (iii) ____________________.

3. The government's budget constraint in the short run is
$G + \_\_\_\_\_ - \text{NET TAX} - \Delta D - \_\_\_\_\_\_\_\_\_\_ = 0.$

4. In the long term the government's budget constraint is
$G - \_\_\_\_\_ = \_\_\_\_\_\_\_\_\_\_ .$

5. The government's fundamental budget constraint is $g - \_\_\_\_\_ = \_\_\_\_\_$.

Problem

Consider the (hypothetical) Balance Sheets of the Fed for two years--1989 and 1990:

$m (end year)	1989	1990
Gold and Foreign Exchange Reserves	100	150
Commercial Banks' Deposits	800	860
Government Securities	900	950
Notes Outstanding	200	240

The government issues coins: $40m were outstanding at the end of 1989 and $44m at the end of 1990.

Calculate:

(a) the monetary base at the end of 1989
(b) the monetary base at the end of 1990
(c) the total amount raised by the inflation tax in 1990
(d) the growth rate of the monetary base in 1990
(e) the amount of taxation deferred by the government by borrowing, if government spending is $1000m and net tax receipts (excluding the inflation tax) are $800m

Project

In your university library, find the latest issue of the Economic Report of the President (Washington, D.C.: U.S. Department of Commerce) and collect the following data for the fiscal years since 1967:

(a) total interest-bearing public debt securities
(b) the total of (a) that is marketable
(c) the total of (a) that is non-marketable
(d) GNP
(e) total government surplus (or deficit)
(f) federal government surplus (or deficit)
(g) state and local government surplus (or deficit)

Calculate the ratio of each of the time series on debt (i.e., (a), (b) and (c)) to GNP. Plot these three series on one graph using a different color for each series. Compare and contrast these three time-series paths.

On another graph plot the three time-series (e), (f) and (g), using a different color for each series. Compare and contrast these three time-series paths.

Answers

Multiple Choice: 1 c 2 b 3 d 4 c 5 b
True or False: 1 T 2 F 3 T 4 F 5 T
Fill in the Blanks:
1. expenditure on goods and services, transfer payments, debt interest payments
2. legislated taxes, net issue of debt, net issue of currency
3. DI, ΔMB
4. T^*, ΔMB
5. t^*, $q(M/P)\cdot\mu$
Problem: (a) \$m1040 (b) \$m1144 (c) \$m104 (d) 10% (e) \$m96

CHAPTER 32

CONTROL OF THE MONEY SUPPLY

When you have completed your study of this chapter you will:

(a) Understand the links between the monetary base and the money supply.
(b) Understand how the Fed operates to achieve its target growth path for the money supply.

Chapter Summary

A. Links Between the Monetary Base and the Money Supply

The money supply function is, like the aggregate supply function, an equilibrium locus. The market that is in equilibrium along the money supply function is the market for monetary base. The demand for monetary base by the general public (the demand for currency) may be presumed to be a fairly stable fraction of the demand for money in total. The demand for monetary base by banks will depend partly on the level of deposits and partly on the market rate of interest. The greater the level of deposits, the more monetary base demanded by banks; the higher the market rate of interest, the smaller the monetary base demanded by banks.

Other things equal, the higher the monetary base, the higher the money supply; and the higher the market rate of interest, the higher the money supply. On the average, the money supply will be a fairly stable multiple of the monetary base, although over shorter periods there will be independent fluctuations in the two variables associated with movements in market rates of interest.

B. Fed's Control of the Money Supply

The Fed seeks to control the money supply by using open market operations to vary the size of the monetary base, thereby inducing changes in the quantity of money.

An alternative technique of monetary control, employed by the Fed until 1979 was to operate on the demand side of the money market. Under that method, the Fed "solved" the demand for money function to determine the level of interest rates that would induce the amount of money demanded to equal the target value of the money supply, given the Fed's own forecasts of the price level and the level of real income. This technique of control is imperfect in the sense that deviations of prices or income from their forecasted values will lead to deviations in the money supply from target.

Multiple Choice

1. a. The money supply is an exact multiple of the monetary base
   b. The higher the interest rate, the higher is the monetary base
   c. If the monetary base falls so too does the money supply
   d. The money supply is only an exact multiple of the monetary base on the average

2. Today, the Fed controls the money supply by controlling:

   a. the monetary base and adjusting interest rates
   b. interest rates on a daily basis
   c. the demand for money
   d. the monetary base so as to achieve its money supply target

3. Until 1979, the Fed controlled the money supply by controlling:

   a. the monetary base and adjusting interest rates
   b. interest rates on a daily basis
   c. the demand for money
   d. the monetary base so as to achieve its money supply target

4. a. Until 1979, the Fed achieved its target for the money supply if its forecasts of real income and the price level were correct
   b. Until 1979, the Fed achieved its target for the money supply by adjusting interest rates so as to balance out errors in its forecasts of real income and the price level
   c. As people are always changing their behavior concerning how much money to hold, it is not surprising that the Fed's attempts at controlling the demand for money were unsuccessful
   d. Until 1979, the Fed attempted to control the money supply by shifting the demand for money function

<u>True or False</u>

1. Given the procedures employed by the Fed, until 1979, for controlling the money supply, a positive random shock to aggregate demand will raise the money supply and by the amount of the demand shock.

2. If, prior to 1979, the Fed made a 10% error in its forecast of the price level but forecasted real income correctly, then the money supply overshot its target by 10%.

3. If, prior to 1979, the Fed made an error in its forecast of real income of 10% but forecasted the price level correctly, then the money supply overshot its target by 10%.

4. Until 1979, the Fed controlled the money supply by controlling interest rates. The way in which the Fed actually moved interest rates up or down to the desired level was by tightening or loosening its hold over the monetary base. For example, if the Fed wanted to raise interest rates then it would sell government securities from its own portfolio to the general public.

5. The Fed now controls the money supply by controlling the monetary base. This is a better technique of control of the money supply than that of manipulation of the demand for money.

6. Controlling the money supply by either the demand for money or directly via the monetary base both involve manipulation of the monetary base.

Fill in the Blanks

1. On the average, the money supply will be a ______________ of the ______________, though over shorter periods there will be ______________ fluctuations in these two variables associated with movements in the ______________________________.

2. The Fed's method of controlling the money supply exploits the link between the ______________ and the ______________. In order to change the size of the monetary base the Fed buys or sells ________________________. When the Fed conducts ____________ ____________ ____________ it changes its assets and thus changes the monetary base.

3. Until 1979, the Fed's method of controlling the money supply was as follows: It ______________ the demand for ______________ function. It then forecasted the ______________ and ______________. It then calculated the ______________ which would make the demand for money equal to the ___________ ______________ ______________. It then conducted open market operations so as to make the ______________ interest rate equal to that calculated.

4. If the Fed, prior to 1979, had correctly forecasted real income but had forecasted too low a price level, interest rates would have been too ____________ and the money supply would have been ____________ the target. Alternatively, if the Fed had correctly forecasted the price level but had forecasted too high a real income level, interest rates would have been too ____________ and the money supply would have been ____________ the target.

Problem

You are given the following information:

1. The quantity of notes and coins held by households and firms is 1/5 of their total holdings of money.
2. The quantity of notes and coins plus deposits with the Fed held by the commercial banks is given by the equation

$$MB_b = \frac{1}{8}D + 700 - 70r_m$$

where MB_b = notes and coins plus deposits with the Fed held by commercial banks

D = bank deposits

r_m = market rate of interest (%)

3. The monetary base is \$300m.

Calculate:

(a) The money supply when $r_m = 10\%$

(b) The money supply when $r_m = 11\%$

(c) The money supply when $r_m = 9\%$

(d) The effect on the money supply of a 1 unit change in the monetary base, holding the market rate of interest constant

(e) The effect on the money supply of a 1 unit change in the market rate of interest, holding the monetary base constant

Answers

Multiple Choice: 1 d 2 d 3 c 4 a

True or False: 1 F 2 T 3 F 4 T 5 T 6 T

Fill in the Blanks:

1. stable multiple, monetary base, independent, market interest rate
2. money supply, monetary base, government securities, open market operations
3. estimated, money, price level, real income, interest rate, money supply target, market
4. low, above, high, below

Problem: (a) \$1000m (b) $\$1233.\dot{3}$m (c) $\$766.\dot{6}$m (d) $\$233.\dot{3}$m (e) $\$3.\dot{3}$m

CHAPTER 33

MONETARY POLICY I: AGGREGATE DEMAND SHOCKS

When you have completed your study of this chapter you will:

(a) Know the key difference between the monetary policy advice given by monetarists and that given by Keynesians.
(b) Know what aggregate demand shocks are and how they affect the aggregate demand curve.
(c) Understand the consequences of following monetarist monetary policy advice in the face of aggregate demand shocks.
(d) Understand the consequences of following Keynesian monetary policy advice in the face of aggregate demand shocks.
(e) Understand why monetarists and Keynesians offer conflicting monetary policy advice.

Chapter Summary

A. Monetarist and Keynesian Monetary Policy Advice

Monetarists recommend the adoption of a steady and predictable money supply growth rule. The money supply growth rate should be kept constant no matter what the current state of the economy.

Keynesians recommend the use of active variations in the money supply to offset aggregate demand shocks. They recommend raising the money supply when output is below its full-employment level and lowering the money supply when output is above its full-employment level.

B. Aggregate Demand Shocks and the Aggregate Demand Curve

Aggregate demand shocks are random variations in the level of aggregate demand which arise from random movements in the timing of expenditures and from random fluctuations in desired holdings of real assets and financial assets. If people try to hold more real assets and fewer financial assets, there will be a rise in the demand for goods--a rise in aggregate demand.

Aggregate demand shocks shift the aggregate demand curve. For any given price level, the level of aggregate demand will vary around its most likely value, depending on the size of the aggregate demand shock.

C. Consequences of Monetarist Policy

Adopting a monetarist policy permits fluctuations in output, employment, unemployment, the price level, the money wage, and the real wage. For example, in the case of a positive aggregate demand shock, output, employment, the price level and the money wage will rise, and the real wage and unemployment will fall.

D. Consequences of Keynesian Policy

Keynesian policy is designed to isolate the economy from a random shock and eliminate fluctuations in output and the price level. In the case of a positive aggregate demand shock, Keynesian monetary policy advice is to lower the money supply so as to leave aggregate demand (and thus the position of the aggregate demand curve) unchanged. This would lead to no adjustment in the rational expectation of the price level, so that the level of output, employment, unemployment, the price level, the real wage and money wage would remain constant.

E. Why Monetarists and Keynesians Offer Conflicting Advice

The dispute between monetarists and Keynesians rests on whether the Fed has an informational advantage over private agents in the economy. Monetarists argue that the Fed has no more information than do private agents. Any attempt by the Fed to offset previous random aggregate demand shocks (now known to all agents in the economy) by varying the money supply will not reduce the fluctuations in output, whereas it will increase those in the price level.

Keynesians assert that the Fed has an effective informational advantage over private agents because private agents get locked into contracts that cannot be revised quickly as new information becomes available. Private agents are locked into contracts based on the wrong expected price level, whereas the Fed can respond quickly to the new information (the aggregate demand shock) and can change the money supply quickly enough so that output, employment, and the price level remain steady.

The successful application of Keynesian policy would require a vast amount of information on the part of the Fed and government, and there is a strong presumption that, in the present state of knowledge they do not have sufficient information. Attempts at pursuing Keynesian policies will be likely to generate bigger fluctuations in both output and price than would the adoption of a monetarist rule.

Multiple Choice

1. Monetary policy advice given by:

   a. Keynesians is to adjust the money supply so as to keep the level of unemployment at zero
   b. Keynesians is to adjust the money supply so as to keep output growing at a constant rate
   c. monetarists is to pick some number and make the growth rate of the money supply equal to that number
   d. monetarists is to keep the money supply growing at a constant known rate each and every year, independent of the level of output

2. Monetary policy advice given by:

   a. Keynesians is aimed at achieving full-employment regardless of the inflationary consequences

b. monetarists is not influenced by the level of unemployment. Monetarists are only interested in conducting monetary policy so as to achieve an inflation goal
c. Keynesians is only relevant in times of recession whereas that given by monetarists is only relevant when the economy is at full-employment
d. monetarists differs from that given by Keynesians because monetarists are interested in the supply side of the economy while Keynesians are concerned with the demand side

3. a. Aggregate demand shocks arise from random government policy
b. Aggregate demand shocks can be positive or negative but most of the time they are zero
c. When a firm predicts a positive random shock it raises output so as to be able to meet the demand for its good
d. If the government was to keep its monetary and fiscal policy steady random aggregate demand shocks would be eliminated

4. In the face of a one-period aggregate demand shock, monetarist monetary policy advice would lead to:

a. higher prices and output forever
b. higher prices and output initially but the steady money supply would lead to a return to price stability in the period following the shock. Output would remain at its now higher level
c. a bigger rise in output than in the price level
d. a rise in both prices and output in the period of the shock but to a return to the initial price and output levels in the period following the shock

5. In the face of a positive one-period aggregate demand shock, Keynesian monetary policy advice would lead to:

a. higher prices and output forever
b. higher prices but no change in output
c. no change in the price level or in output
d. a fall in the price level but no change in output

6. Keynesian monetary policy advice with no informational advantage in the face of a negative one-period aggregate demand shock leads to:

a. a fall in the price level but no change in output
b. a path for the price level and for output which is identical to that that would be achieved by following monetarist monetary policy advice
c. fluctuations in the price level that are larger than the fluctuations in the price level that would be achieved using monetarist monetary policy advice
d. fluctuations in output that are smaller than those that would be generated by monetarist monetary policy advice

<u>True or False</u>

1. The essence of the dispute between Keynesians and monetarists concerning the effects of monetary policy turn on the question of information and the use that may be made of new information.

2. Keynesians assert that the Fed has an effective informational advantage. They assert that individuals get locked into contracts based on an expected price level that, after the fact of an aggregate demand shock, turns out to be wrong. The Fed can act, after private agents have tied themselves into contractual arrangements, to compensate for and offset the effects of random shocks.

3. Keynesian monetary policy advice, by its description, implies that Keynesians are willing to use unanticipated changes in the money supply in order to influence the real variables in the economy.

4. If monetarist monetary policy advice was followed the only things that can lead to business cycles are random fluctuations arising from private aggregate demand (or aggregate supply) shocks.

5. Monetarists are simply too ignorant about the workings of the economy to enable them to do any better than to remove at least some of the sources of fluctuation in economic activity. Keynesians, on the other hand, are much better informed about how the economy actually functions. It makes much more sense to follow Keynesian monetary policy advice than that of monetarists.

Fill in the Blanks

1. Aggregate demand shocks are ___________ variations in the level of ___________ ___________ that arise from ___________ movements in the ___________ of private agents' expenditures and ___________ fluctuations in their ___________ holdings of real and financial assets.

2. Monetarist policy is designed to allow fluctuations in all macroeconomic variables in response to ___________ ___________ ___________. Monetarist monetary policy is designed to ___________ fluctuations in all macroeconomic variables arising from ___________ ___________ in the ___________ ___________.

3. Monetarists argue that the Fed has _____ ___________ informational advantage over private agents. Any attempt the Fed makes to offset previous ___________ aggregate demand shocks now known to private agents will not ___________ fluctuations in output and will only ___________ fluctuations in the ___________ ___________.

4. Keynesian policy advice rests on the assertion that the Fed has an ___________ informational advantage over ___________ ___________ that enables the Fed to respond to random shocks while private agents are locked into ___________ so as to ___________ the impact of the shock.

5. In order to conduct Keynesian monetary policy successfully, a vast amount of __________ about the economy is required by the __________. In the present state of knowledge, there is a strong __________ that the Fed does _____ have __________ __________.

6. If the Fed does not have an effective informational advantage over __________ __________ in the face of an aggregate demand shock, then the path for __________ and __________ is the same under both Keynesian and monetarist monetary policy but the path for the _______ _______ is _______ volatile if Keynesian monetary policy rather than monetarist monetary policy is adopted.

Answers

Multiple Choice: 1 d 2 a 3 b 4 d 5 c 6 c
True or False: 1 T 2 T 3 T 4 T 5 F
Fill in the Blanks:
1. random, aggregate demand, random, timing, random, desired
2. aggregate demand shocks, eliminate, unanticipated fluctuations, money supply
3. no effective, random, reduce, increase, price level
4. effective, private agents, contracts, offset
5. information, Fed, presumption, not, sufficient information
6. private agents, output, employment, price level, more

CHAPTER 34

MONETARY POLICY II: AGGREGATE SUPPLY SHOCKS

When you have completed your study of this chapter you will:

(a) Understand how a supply shock affects the production function, the real wage and levels of employment and unemployment, and the aggregate supply curve.
(b) Understand the distinction between the expectations-augmented aggregate supply curve and the expectation of the aggregate supply curve.
(c) Understand the consequences of following monetarist policy advice in the event of an aggregate supply shock.
(d) Understand the consequences of following Keynesian policy advice in the event of an aggregate supply shock.
(e) Understand the consequences of following a Keynesian policy with an information lag.
(f) Understand the essence of the dispute and why there is a further presumption in favor of monetarism.

Chapter Summary

A. Effects of Supply Shocks

A negative aggregate supply shock lowers the amount of output which can be produced at each level of labor input. It also lowers the marginal productivity of labor and shifts the demand for labor curve downwards. The new equilibrium in the labor market following a negative aggregate supply shock is one with a lower real wage and a lower level of employment. There may be a temporary rise in the measured unemployment rate as people who were previously in employment seek alternative occupations. The aggregate supply curve shifts leftward, partly as a result of the production function shift, and partly as a result of the reduced equilibrium level of employment.

B. Expectations-Augmented Aggregate Supply Curve and the Expectation of the Aggregate Supply Curve

The expectations-augmented aggregate supply curve traces the amount of aggregate supply as the price level varies for a given expected price level. The expectation of the aggregate supply curve refers to the vertical aggregate supply curve, which traces the quantity that will be supplied at each price level when the price level is fully expected. The expectation of that vertical aggregate supply curve refers to its position in normal or usual periods, when aggregate supply shocks are zero.

C. Consequences of Monetarist Policy

A random negative shock to aggregate supply with a fixed money supply will lower the level of output and raise the price level in the period in which the aggregate supply shock occurs. The level of employment will fall. The economy will experience stagflation.

D. Consequences of Keynesian Policy

Keynesian policy in the face of a negative aggregate supply shock would be to stimulate demand by raising the money supply. Perfectly conducted, this would have the effect of leaving output and employment unchanged, but raising the price level.

E. Consequences of Keynesian Policy with an Information Lag

If a Keynesian policy is followed but with a one-period lag in the receipt of information concerning the aggregate supply shock, the economy would respond in exactly the same way under a Keynesian policy as it would have done under a monetarist policy in the period in which the shock occurs. If, using a Keynesian policy, the monetary authorities stimulate demand with a one-period lag and if everyone correctly anticipates this, there will be a rise in the price level but no output effect in the second period.

F. The Essence of the Dispute and Why There Is a Further Presumption in Favor of Monetarism

The essence of the dispute between Keynesians and monetarists concerning the appropriate response to aggregate supply shocks is exactly the same as that discussed in the previous chapter concerning aggregate demand shocks. The issue turns on who gets information fastest and who can react fastest to new information. If the Fed has no superior information, then the use of Keynesian policy to correct aggregate supply shocks will leave the behavior of output unaffected and will produce a greater degree of price level variability than will the pursuit of a monetarist rule.

Multiple Choice

1. A negative aggregate supply shock:

   a. lowers the production function, shifts the aggregate supply curve to the left but has no effect on the labor market
   b. reduces the demand for labor so that there is a fall in the real wage, marginal product of labor, employment and aggregate output
   c. shifts the aggregate supply curve to the left, lowers output and raises the real wage
   d. lowers the real wage and raises the supply of labor

2. A negative aggregate supply shock:

   a. moves the EAS curve to the right
   b. makes the EAS curve steeper
   c. drags the EAS curve to the left
   d. does not affect the EAS curve

3. Monetarist monetary policy advice in the face of a positive aggregate supply shock:

   a. raises the price level and output
   b. lowers the price level but raises output
   c. lowers the price level and lowers output
   d. raises the price level and lowers output

4. Keynesian monetary policy advice in the face of a positive aggregate supply shock:

   a. avoids both stagflation and a deflationary boom
   b. leads to stagflation
   c. leads to deflation
   d. leads to inflation

5. If there is no informational advantage, a temporary aggregate supply shock will have:

   a. smaller effects on output if Keynesian policy is followed
   b. larger price level effects if the government does nothing
   c. smaller price level effects if monetarist policy advice is followed
   d. no effect on the price level if the correct mix of monetarist and Keynesian monetary policy is followed

<u>True or False</u>

1. The expectation of the aggregate supply curve is the same as the expectations-augmented aggregate supply curve.

2. An aggregate supply shock shifts the AS curve but does not affect the position of the EAS curve.

3. A random shock to aggregate supply leads private agents to revise their expectation of the price level and so the EAS curve moves with the AS curve.

4. In the event of a supply shock Keynesian monetary policy advice with an information lag leads to greater instability in the economy than would be the case if a monetarist monetary policy rule had been followed.

5. Keynesian policy advice is always directed towards keeping the unemployment rate at its natural rate. Irrespective of whether the shock to the economy is an aggregate supply shock or an aggregate demand shock Keynesians are not bothered by the inflationary consequences of their monetary policy advice.

<u>Fill in the Blanks</u>

1. A negative shock to aggregate supply with a fixed money supply __________ output and __________ and __________ the price level.

2. The expectation of the AS curve is the AS curve in __________ or __________ periods when __________ __________ __________ are zero.

3. A negative shock to aggregate supply shifts the _____ curve to the __________ and drags with it the _____ curve. The intersection of these two curves remains at the __________ __________ of the __________ __________ .

4. A negative shock to aggregate supply __________ the production function, __________ the marginal product of labor, shifts the demand for labor to the __________, __________ the real wage and __________ employment.

5. Keynesian monetary policy leads to __________ fluctuations in the price level than does monetarist monetary policy, if there is no __________ __________ .

Problems

1. If an aggregate supply shock lowers aggregate supply by 10% when expected and actual aggregate demand are constant, what is the change in output? Does the price level rise or fall? What does the magnitude of the change in the price level depend upon?

2. If there is a positive aggregate demand shock which is 5% of full-employment output, and the money supply is correctly expected to be raised 5%, calculate the change in the expected price level, the actual price level, and output.

Answers

Multiple Choice: 1 b 2 c 3 b 4 a 5 c
True or False: 1 F 2 F 3 F 4 T 5 T
Fill in the Blanks:
1. lowers, employment, raises
2. normal, usual, aggregate supply shocks
3. AS, left, EAS, rational expectation, price level
4. lowers, lowers, left, lowers, lowers
5. greater, informational advantage
Problems:
1. 10%, fall, the slope of the EAS curve
2. 5%, >5%, 5%

CHAPTER 35

FISCAL POLICY

When you have completed your study of this chapter you will:

(a) Understand the key differences between the Keynesian and monetarist policy recommendations concerning fiscal policy.
(b) Understand the distinction between anticipated and unanticipated fiscal policy.
(c) Know how output, employment, unemployment, the real wage, money wage, and price level are affected by an anticipated change in government expenditure.
(d) Know how output, employment, unemployment, the real wage, money wage, and price level are affected by an unanticipated change in government expenditure.

Chapter Summary

A. Monetarist and Keynesian Fiscal Policy Advice

Keynesians recommend the active use of variations in government spending and taxes to raise aggregate demand when output is below its full-employment level and to lower aggregate demand when output is above its full-employment level.

Monetarists urge the maintaining of a steady fiscal policy that is dictated by resource allocation considerations between the public and private sector, and not by economic stabilization considerations. They advocate a level of government spending consistent with an optimal division of resources between the government and private sector, and a level of taxes such that the money supply growth target which they advocate may be achieved.

B. Anticipated and Unanticipated Fiscal Policy

Just as in the case of monetary policy, a change in government expenditure or taxes may be decomposed into that part which was anticipated and that part which was unanticipated. The unanticipated change in government spending and taxes is simply the actual change minus the change that was anticipated. When there is no unanticipated change, fiscal policy is anticipated.

C. The Effects of an Anticipated Change in Government Expenditure

An anticipated rise in government expenditure matched by an equal anticipated tax rise will raise the price level and raise the money wage by the same percentage amount. It will leave the level of output, employment, unemployment, and the real wage unchanged. These predictions assume neutral tax changes.

D. The Effects of an Unanticipated Change in Government Expenditure

An unanticipated rise in government expenditure matched by an equal unanticipated tax rise will raise the level of output and the price level. It will also raise the level of employment and the money wage. However, the money wage will not rise by as much as the price level, and the real wage will fall. There will also be a fall in the unemployment rate.

Exactly the same considerations apply to evaluating the appropriateness of alternative fiscal policies as were discussed in Chapters 33 and 34 (pp. 475-500 of the textbook) concerning monetary policies. That material should be studied carefully and its relevance to the fiscal policy debate understood.

Multiple Choice

1. Fiscal policy:

   a. is policy concerning the level of government expenditure and taxation
   b. includes job creation programs that are designed to raise the level of employment and that are financed by money printing
   c. includes the setting of minimum wages so that all workers can receive at least a fair wage
   d. includes unemployment insurance programs that are designed to be self-financing and that protect workers who are laid off

2. a. Keynesians advocate the use of expansionary fiscal policy to keep the level of aggregate demand rising
   b. Monetarists advocate that the level of government expenditure and taxes be set so that the unemployment rate is at its natural rate and then to be held constant and announced so that every agent in the economy knows exactly what fiscal policy is
   c. Keynesians advocate the use of fiscal policy to maintain a zero unemployment rate in the economy
   d. Monetarist fiscal policy advice concerns the optimal allocation of resources between the private and the public sector. The level of government expenditure should be set so that the marginal utility per dollar spent on public goods is equal to the marginal utility per dollar spent on private goods. The level of taxation should be set, given a constant rate of growth of the money supply that will deliver low inflation, so as to balance the government's budget

3. a. An anticipated rise in government expenditure and taxes increases job opportunities and so raises the demand for labor and the real wage
   b. An unanticipated rise in government spending and taxes raises the price level, employment and output, and lowers unemployment and the real wage
   c. An unanticipated change in government expenditure leads to a revision of the expected price level and a shift of the EAS curve
   d. An anticipated change in government expenditure raises the price level. The rise in the price level is independent of whether the rise in government expenditure is financed by taxes or money printing

True or False

1. An anticipated rise in government spending matched by an equal anticipated rise in taxes has no effect on the level of output or prices.

2. If everyone (government and private agents) could correctly and precisely anticipate all shocks to the economy then output would always be at its full-employment level and there would be no role for Keynesian fiscal policy but there would be a role for Keynesian monetary policy in order to stabilize the price level.

3. If the government budget deficit is expected to rise by 10% but actually falls by 10% there will be a fall in output and employment, a rise in the real wage but the price level may fall or rise.

4. A permanent tax cut not matched by a cut in government spending will raise the rate of inflation.

5. An anticipated and permanent rise in government expenditure not matched by a tax rise will have no effect on output but will raise the inflation rate initially and then it would come down in subsequent years to a steady-state value that exceeds the original inflation rate.

Fill in the Blanks

1. ___________ advocate active use of fiscal policy to keep output at its full-employment level. Monetarists advocate setting the level of ___________ ___________ such that the allocation of resources are economically ___________ and ___________ of the state of unemployment or ___________; and the setting of taxes such that given the rate of growth of the money supply, the budget is ___________.

2. Anticipated rises in fiscal policy raise the ___________ and leave ___________ unchanged. This implies that for Keynesian fiscal policy to be effective it must be ___________.

Problem

Assume an economy in which the steady-state rate of growth of output is 3% per annum, and the existing trends in monetary and fiscal policy are such that the steady-state inflation rate is 10% per annum. For the coming year there are strong fears arising from the size of the government's budget deficit that the money supply growth rate will accelerate to 18% per annum. At the same time, the Fed puts a tight rein on monetary growth lowering it unexpectedly to 8% per annum. Calculate:

(a) the expected inflation rate
(b) the actual inflation rate
(c) the rate of growth of output

If in the above problem when the Fed tightens the rein on monetary policy there is also a negative aggregate supply shock which lowers the rate of growth of full-employment output to 2% per annum:

(d) What is now the expected inflation rate?
(e) Compare the actual inflation rate with that in (b) above
(f) What is now the rate of growth of output?

If in the above problem there is a shock to aggregate demand which reduces it by a further 1 percentage point, but there is no supply shock, calculate:

(g) the expected inflation rate
(h) the actual inflation rate
(i) the growth rate of output

Answers

Multiple Choice: 1 a 2 d 3 b
True or False: 1 F 2 F 3 T 4 T 5 T
Fill in the Blanks:
1. Keynesians, government spending, efficient, independent, output, balanced
2. price level, output, unanticipated
Problem: (a) 15% (b) $5\% < \pi < 15\%$ (c) $-7\% < \rho < 3\%$ (d) 15% (e) lower (f) $-8 < \rho < 2\%$ (g) 15% (h) $4\% < \pi < 15\%$ (i) $-8 < \rho < 3\%$

CHAPTER 36

WAGE AND PRICE CONTROLS

When you have completed your study of this chapter you will:

(a) Know the main features of the content of a wage and price control program.
(b) Understand the distinction between a posted price and an actual price.
(c) Understand why wage and price controls do not affect the expected price level.
(d) Understand why wage and price controls do not affect the actual price level.
(e) Understand why wage and price controls can only make matters worse.

Chapter Summary

A. Content of a Wage and Price Control Program

A wage and price control program has three features:

1. Rules about wages, prices, and profits.
2. Sanctions and penalties.
3. A monitoring agency.

B. Posted Price and Actual Price

A posted price is the published or announced price; an actual price is the price at which a trade actually takes place for a given quantity and quality of the product (or factor service).

C. Wage and Price Controls and the Expected Price Level

Since wage and price controls do not (as a first approximation) affect the level of the money supply or the level of government spending, they do not affect the level of aggregate demand. Also, as a first approximation, they do not affect aggregate supply. Since they do not therefore affect anything that determines the actual price level, it would be irrational to expect the actual price level to be affected by controls.

D. Wage and Price Controls and the Actual Price Level

The actual price level is determined at the intersection of the aggregate demand and expectations-augmented aggregate supply curves. Wage and price controls do not shift either of these curves and do not therefore affect the actual price level.

E. Wage and Price Controls Make Matters Worse

To the extent that wage and price controls divert resources from the private sector, they lower output and raise the price level. To the extent that they generate a bigger government spending level to finance, they raise the price level. To the extent that they encourage slack monetary policies, they raise the inflation rate. To the extent that wage and price controls are applied unevenly and made to stick in some sectors, they generate relative price distortions and produce losses of economic welfare from a misallocation of resources.

Multiple Choice

1. A wage and price control program is a program that:

   a. reduces the economy-wide average money wage
   b. reduces the price level
   c. raises employment
   d. has, at best, no effect on the economy

2. A wage and price control program:

   a. diverts resources from the private sector
   b. raises output and lowers the price level
   c. affects all sectors of the economy evenly
   d. does not produce a loss of economic welfare

3. Wage and price controls:

   a. are the modern technique for controlling inflation
   b. are favored by firms because they limit the extent of wage rises and they are favored by households as they lower inflation
   c. are a facade behind which the Fed can conduct slack monetary policy
   d. do not affect aggregate supply but they do lower aggregate demand so that the rational expectation of the price level is lowered

True or False

1. Wage and price controls do lower the rate of inflation because people adjust their expectations of inflation in line with the controls.

2. Wage and price controls are most often useless but when the economy is experiencing stagflation they are of great use.

3. Wage and price controls reduce the loss of welfare from inflation.

4. Wage and price controls will lead to a rise in inflation if the Fed now considers it is not responsible for the inflation rate and pursues policy of rapid monetary growth.

5. If the expectation is that the price level will rise, wage and price controls can do little to keep the price level constant.

6. Wage and price controls are harmful because they lead to a misallocation of resources between industries as well as between the private and government sectors.

7. In year 0 the growth rate of real income was 2% below trend and inflation was running at 10% per annum. In year 1 the government introduces a wage and price control program which allows wages and prices to rise at 5% per annum. Inflation and output remain the same in year 1 if the wage and

price control program was unanticipated but in year 2 inflation falls and output rises.

8. In an industry where wages and prices are strictly controlled by the monitoring agency set up as part of a wage and price control program, consumers of this good have higher welfare than otherwise because the price of this good does not rise as quickly as other prices.

9. Under a program of wage and price controls the government sets controls on the prices at which all transactions in goods and labor take place and polices these prices. It is a useful tool which allows the government to choose the inflation rate.

10. Wage and price controls at best have no effect on inflation and unemployment and probably even raise both of these.

Fill in the Blanks

1. A wage and price control program has three features: (i) ____________ about ____________, ____________ and ____________; (ii) ____________ and (iii) a ____________ ____________.

2. Wage and price controls attempt to control ____________ prices and not the ____________ prices at which trades take place. They make no attempt to control the ____________ or ____________ of a transaction.

3. Wage and price controls do not ____________ the ____________ price level. They may actually ____________ the inflation rate and ____________ output.

Problem

An economy has been experiencing an inflation rate of 10% per annum and in year 0, everyone expects inflation of 10%, with 10% growth in the money supply to occur in year 1. In year 1, the government imposes wage and price controls designed to limit inflation to 5% per annum. Also, the money supply growth rate is lowered but unexpectedly so, to a level that makes aggregate demand rise by only 5% per annum.

Calculate:

(a) the expected inflation rate in year 1
(b) the actual inflation rate in year 1
(c) the actual output growth rate in year 1

Answers

Multiple Choice: 1 d 2 a 3 c
True or False: 1 F 2 F 3 F 4 T 5 T 6 T 7 F 8 F 9 F 10 T
Fill in the Blanks:
1. rules, wages, prices, profits, penalties, monitoring agency
2. posted, actual, quality, quantity
3. lower, expected, raise, lower
Problem: (a) 10% (b) $5\% < \pi < 10\%$ (c) $-5\% < \rho < 0\%$

CHAPTER 37

U.S. MACROECONOMIC POLICY

This chapter deals with U.S macroeconomic policy in the period beginning with the election of President Truman at the end of 1948 and running through successive administrations of Presidents Eisenhower, Kennedy, Johnson, Nixon, Ford and Carter, and ending at the middle of the current term of President Reagan. When you have completed your study of this chapter you will:

(a) Know the main features of monetary policy.
(b) Know the main features of fiscal policy.
(c) Know the contents of the wage and price control programs.
(d) Understand how each of these policies has contributed to the performance of inflation, unemployment, and output.
(e) Know the economic policies and performance of each administration from Truman to Reagan and be able to compare and evaluate these policies.

Chapter Summary

A. Monetary Policy

U.S. monetary policy may be summarized by examining the growth rate of the money supply. After a strong burst of monetary growth in the early 1950s, there was a general downward trend in its rate that persisted until 1960. Since then, the money supply has grown increasingly quickly on the average. There have been clear cycles in the growth rate of the money supply, ranging from two to seven years, and averaging four years. The money supply growth rate has been volatile, and there is no appearance of reduced volatility in its rate in the years since monetary targeting was introduced in 1975.

B. Fiscal Policy

Whether measured in "actual" or "high-employment" terms, the federal government has been taking an increasing fraction of GNP in the post-war years, although the decline in military spending following the Korean War was the dominant influence on fiscal policy in the 1950s. Taxes have not increased as quickly as expenditure, however, and the deficit has gradually grown. There have been clear cycles in fiscal policy averaging five years in duration. Fiscal policy was particularly tight (or contractionary) during 1958-1960 and loose (or expansionary) during 1965-1968.

C. Wage and Price Controls

"Guideposts" were employed in the Kennedy years and "Price and Pay Standards" during the Carter years. The only full-blown mandatory wage and price control program was the Economic Stabilization Program of Richard Nixon, which ran from 1971 to 1974. The program had four phases, the first of which was an outright freeze and the remaining phases of which were designed to hold wage increases to 5.5% and price increases to 2.5%.

D. Policy and Performance

Decomposing the growth rate of the money supply into its anticipated and unanticipated components makes it possible to look at the extent to which these two separate parts of monetary policy have influenced the economy. Trends in the anticipated growth rate of the money supply, themselves generated by trends in fiscal policy and in unemployment, seem clearly capable of accounting for the trends in inflation. Unanticipated variations in money supply growth appear to account for the fluctuations of real GNP about its trend. Some of its fluctuations, however, that actually occurred are more extreme than can be explained on the basis of only unanticipated money growth. These occurred in 1958-1961 (below trend) and 1965-1968 (above trend). Major swings in fiscal policy seem to be able to make some contribution to understanding these movements of real GNP.

Wage and price controls probably had very little effect either on wages or prices, after induced changes in quality and mismeasurement of the normal aggregate price indexes are allowed for.

E. Comparison of Administrations--Truman to Reagan

In narrow macroeconomic terms--as judged by inflation and unemployment--the Eisenhower administration turned in the best performance in the post-war years. All administrations since then have presided over rising inflation and (with the exception of Kennedy-Johnson), rising unemployment. Regardless of the political party forming the administration, both government spending and the deficit have trended upwards. There does not appear to be any significant difference between political parties concerning the way in which they manage the economy. With only two years of evidence in so far, it is too early to judge whether that statement will be applicable to the Reagan administration. On current showing it appears that it will.

Multiple Choice

1. The four distinct eras of monetary policymaking in the United States since World War II include:

   a. the first phase in which the dollar was "as good as gold" and U.S. citizens could buy gold from the Fed at $35 per ounce
   b. the second phase ran from the end of the fixed exchange rate period (1971) to the beginning of the flexible exchange rate period (1975)
   c. the third phase, beginning in 1975, was a period of monetary targeting with interest rate control
   d. the fourth phase involved no monetary targeting but use of open market operations so as to influence the interest rate

2. The U.S. money supply growth rate:

   a. has been on a rising trend since 1950
   b. was on a falling trend to 1970 and a rising trend after that date
   c. was on a falling trend to 1960 and a rising trend after that date
   d. displays distinct cycles of constant duration of four years

3. The main features of U.S. fiscal policy since 1949 include:

   a. a rising deficit as a result of taxes falling and federal spending remaining fairly steady
   b. a constant ratio of high-employment federal spending to capacity output
   c. a rising trend in the fraction of GNP that the federal government spends
   d. a rise in taxes which is faster than the rise in federal spending expressed as a fraction of GNP

4. Wage and price controls:

   a. have never been used in the United States
   b. were implemented for the first time by the Carter administration
   c. were used by Truman to control post-war inflation
   d. have been tried many times but never with the thoroughness and severity of the Nixon program

5. Anticipated M1 growth is larger:

   a. the larger the current year's unemployment rate
   b. the larger the current year's level of federal government spending
   c. the smaller the two previous years' M1 growth
   d. the larger current years' level of federal government spending relative to its trend

6. Deviations of real GNP from trend are accounted for:

   a. entirely by anticipated fiscal policy changes
   b. mainly by unanticipated money supply growth
   c. labor market shocks that cause bigger fluctuations in unemployment about the natural rate
   d. predictable changes in the government's deficit

7. Since 1949 economic performance of the United States was better under the Eisenhower administration than any other, because on the average:

   a. unemployment was lower
   b. federal spending as a percent of GNP was higher
   c. the federal budget was closer to being balanced
   d. inflation was lower

<u>True or False</u>

1. Monetary targeting was implemented with a constant money supply growth rate established in 1975 and maintained ever since. Thus, U.S. monetary targeting is a good test of monetarism.

2. In 1975, monetary targeting was implemented by a system of indirect money stock control through the manipulation of interest rates.

3. At the beginning of the Kennedy-Johnson administration inflation was low and unemployment high, but at the end inflation was high and unemployment was low.

4. The major fiscal policy change in the second half of the 1970s has been the emergence of a large surplus in the government's budget.

5. Wage and price controls cannot control wages, prices and profits at the same time. They can only attempt to control two of these.

6. The slowdown in inflation during the Nixon wage and price control program was mainly and unambiguously the result of the wage and price control program.

7. The slowdown of inflation under the Reagan administration has been accompanied by a higher unemployment rate and government deficit.

<u>Fill in the Blanks</u>

1. Monetary and fiscal policy can explain the ____________ ____________ in inflation in the United States in the post-war years and can also account for most of the ____________ in real economic activity.

2. ____________________money growth has been a dominant influence on ____________ of real income from trend.

3. Extensions of coverage of unemployment insurance have increased the ____________ ______ ______ ____________ .

4. The four different eras of monetary policy are: the first from 1946 to ____________, the United States was operating on a ____________ ____________ ____________; the second era from __________ to __________ represents the hiatus between the end of the ____________ ____________ ____________ and the beginning of ____________ ____________; the third era is a period of ____________ ____________ with ____________ ____________ ____________; and since __________ the Fed has conducted ____________ ____________ with ____________ management of the ____________ ____________ .

<u>Answers</u>

<u>Multiple Choice</u>: 1 c 2 c 3 c 4 d 5 d 6 b 7 d
<u>True or False</u>: 1 F 2 F 3 T 4 F 5 T 6 F 7 T
<u>Fill in the Blanks</u>:
1. broad trends, cycles
2. unanticipated, deviations
3. natural rate of unemployment
4. 1971, gold exchange standard, 1971, 1975, gold exchange standard, monetary targeting, monetary targeting, interest rate control, 1979, monetary targeting, direct, monetary base

CHAPTER 38

LONG-TERM TREND IN OUTPUT

This chapter introduces the next part of the book--Growth and Supply side. So far, most of the material that you have studied in this textbook has abstracted from long-term trends and has been concerned with understanding the fluctuations around the trend. This chapter will help you understand what determines the trend itself.

When you have completed your study of this chapter you will:

(a) Understand the concept of the per capita production function.
(b) Know how to represent per capita output and savings in a simple diagram.
(c) Understand the concept of the steady-state investment rate.
(d) Know how to find the equilibrium values of per capita output, capital, consumption, savings, and investment.
(e) Understand what determines the trend rate of growth of output.

Chapter Summary

A. The Per Capita Production Function

The per capita production function shows the maximum amount of per capita production obtainable as the capital-labor ratio is increased. The per capita production function will shift over time as a result of technical change.

B. Per Capita Output and Savings

Per capita savings (which is the same thing as per capita capital accumulation) would be some fraction of per capita output. Thus, the rate of per capita capital accumulation depends on the level of capital per head.

C. Steady-State Investment Rate

Because the per capita rate of capital accumulation depends on the capital-labor ratio, it follows that, in general, at any given capital-labor ratio, there will be a tendency for the capital-labor ratio to either rise or fall. The steady-state investment rate is the rate of investment (of capital accumulation) that maintains the capital-labor ratio constant. The investment rate that maintains the capital-labor ratio constant is the capital-labor ratio multiplied by the population growth rate.

D. Equilibrium Per Capita Output, Capital, Consumption, Savings, and Investment

The equilibrium value of the capital-labor ratio is determined by the capital-labor ratio that generates a volume of savings per head equal to the steady-state rate of investment per head. When savings per head equal steady-state investment per head, the capital-labor ratio, output per head, consumption per head, and savings per head are all constant.

E. Determinants of the Trend Rate of Growth of Output

The trend rate of growth of output is determined by the population growth rate and the rate of technical change. It does not depend on the savings rate. If the savings rate changes, however, there is a transition from one level of output per head to another that involves a change in the growth rate. Specifically, a rise in the savings rate raises the capital-labor ratio and output per head. A fall in the population growth rate also has these same effects. Per capita consumption is maximized when the marginal product of capital equals the population growth rate. This is known as the "golden rule". There is a unique saving rate that will deliver the golden rule. Too much savings relative to the golden rule will produce a higher output per head but a lower consumption per head than the golden rule value.

Multiple Choice

1. The per capita production function:

   a. shows how much output a given amount of capital per head can produce
   b. is a constant function of the capital-labor ratio
   c. shows the per capita output that various capital-labor ratios can produce
   d. is the aggregate production function divided by the number of people employed

2. The steady-state rate of investment is not:

   a. the rate of investment which maintains a constant capital-labor ratio
   b. equal to per capita savings
   c. equal to the rate of population growth
   d. the rate of investment that maintains a constant capital stock

3. The golden rule is:

   a. a far-fetched goal
   b. that the rate of savings equals the rate of population growth
   c. that the marginal product of capital equals the rate of population growth
   d. a rule to be used in the short run to raise output per head

4. The trend growth rate of output is:

   a. equal to the population growth rate
   b. such that per capita consumption equals per capita savings
   c. such that the capital-labor ratio is growing at the population growth rate
   d. such that the stock of capital is constant

True or False

1. The growth rate of output depends on the growth rate of population and on the rate of technical change.

2. The level of output per head and the capital-labor ratio depend on both the population growth rate and the savings rate.

3. The golden rule is the rate of savings which maximizes output per head.

4. The trend rate of growth of output does not depend on the savings rate.

5. Per capita consumption is maximized when the marginal product of capital equals the population growth rate.

6. There is a unique saving rate that delivers the golden rule.

Fill in the Blanks

1. The per capita production function shows the ____________ amount of per capita ____________ obtainable as the __________________ ratio is increased. The per capita production function will shift over time as a result of ____________ ____________ .

2. Per capita savings would be some ____________ of per capita output. Thus, the rate of per capita ____________ ____________ depends on the level of capital per head.

3. The investment rate that maintains the capital-labor ratio constant is the ____________ ratio multiplied by the ____________ ____________ ____________ .

4. When savings per head equal steady-state investment per head, the ____________ ratio, output per head, ____________ per head, and savings per head are all constant.

5. There is a ____________ saving rate that will deliver the golden rule. Too much savings relative to the ____________ ____________ will produce a ____________ output per head but a ____________ consumption per head than the golden rule value.

Answers

Multiple Choice: 1 c 2 d 3 c 4 a
True or False: 1 T 2 T 3 F 4 T 5 T 6 T
Fill in the Blanks
1. maximum, output, capital-labor, technical change
2. fraction, capital accumulation
3. capital-labor, population growth rate
4. capital-labor, consumption
5. unique, golden rule, higher, lower

CHAPTER 39

THE "SUPPLY SIDE"

When you have completed your study of this chapter you will:

(a) Understand why governments are productive.
(b) Understand how productive government activity affects the production function and the demand for labor.
(c) Understand how paying for government (taxation) affects the supply of labor.
(d) Understand how efficient government raises output and employment.
(e) Understand how overgrown government lowers output and employment.
(f) Know the effects of supply-side policies on the price level.
(g) Understand how the supply-side analysis can be extended to apply to savings and capital accumulation.
(h) Know the supply-side policies of the Reagan administration.

Chapter Summary

A. Why Governments Are Productive

Governments are productive because, by using their monopoly in coercion, they are able to reduce the resources involved in protection of persons and property and are able to enforce public health standards that raise the productivity of labor. Governments do many other things that are productive, but there is controversy and imprecise knowledge concerning the productivity of these additional government activities as compared with the productivity of equivalent privately provided services. In addition, governments indulge in many activities that have either low or perhaps even negative productivity.

B. How Productive Government Activity Affects the Production Function and the Demand for Labor

Productive government activity can be viewed as shifting the production function upwards so that higher output levels are attainable at each level of labor input. Similarly, the slope of the production function is increased or, equivalently, the marginal product of labor rises. This means that the demand for labor curve shifts upwards.

C. How Taxes Affect the Supply of Labor

The higher the taxes, the lower will be the supply of labor. The supply of labor will depend on the after-tax real wage. In general, the higher the after-tax real wage, the more labor will be supplied. Thus, a rise in taxes that lowers the after-tax wage rate will cause the labor supply curve to shift to the left.

D. How Efficient Government Raises Output and Employment

The efficient government raises output, employment, and real wages as a result of the operation of two offsetting forces, one of which clearly dominates. The dominant force is the rise in the production function and the rise in the demand for labor that results from the provision of productive government activity. To some degree offsetting this, although only partially so, is the effect of the taxes levied to pay for the government services. These lower the supply of labor. Nevertheless, the two effects combined (Figure 39.3 on p. 570 of the textbook) result in higher output, higher employment, and higher real wages.

E. How Overgrown Government Lowers Output and Employment

Government can grow too big in the sense that taxes continue to be increased and to be spent on activities that do not raise the production function and the marginal product of labor. When this happens, all the effects of increased government size are negative, and the supply of labor curve shifts to the left, thereby producing a lower level of employment, lower output, and a lower after-tax real wage (Figure 39.4 on p. 572 of the textbook).

F. The Effects of Supply-Side Policies on the Price Level

Any action that shifts the aggregate supply curve will, other things given, change the price level in the opposite direction. Thus, a rise in output (shifting aggregate supply to the right), resulting from supply-side policies, lowers the price level. Supply-side policies in and of themselves have no effect on the rate of inflation, which is determined by the growth rate of the money supply.

G. Extension of Supply-Side Analysis to Savings and Capital Accumulation

The supply-side analysis applied in this chapter to the labor market could be applied equally well to the market for capital goods and the supply of savings. Just as higher taxes on labor income are a disincentive to work, so high taxes on capital income are a disincentive to save. Lower savings result in lower capital accumulation and lower output. As an empirical matter, the importance of these effects is in dispute and is badly in need of detailed numerical measurement.

H. Reagan's Supply-Side Policies

The supply-side policies of the Reagan administration involve increasing defense spending, cutting spending on domestic programs, cutting taxes, and deregulating. In terms of the analysis of this chapter, this should be thought of as attempting to raise productive government spending and to cut unproductive government spending, thereby shifting the production function upwards. Tax cuts are designed to shift the supply of labor (and supply of savings) curves to the right. Deregulation is like cutting both taxes and government spending simultaneously. The hoped-for effects of these policies is a rise in output and employment. It is recognized that these effects will occur in the long term and that in the short term there will be a rise in the federal budget deficit. However, there are good reasons to believe that the short term may well last for a long time, so that the hoped-for effects may be so long in coming that the short-run budget deficit triggers a renewed burst of inflation in the intervening period. The policies would be more convincingly pursued with more vigorous cutting of unproductive government activity and a balanced federal budget.

Multiple Choice

1. The government is more productive than the private sector at supplying the following activities:

   a. the redistribution of income
   b. the provision of basic legal and security system
   c. the redistribution of wealth
   d. the provision of social security

2. A rise in the level of productive government activities:

   a. shifts the production function upwards
   b. makes the slope of the production function flatter
   c. shifts the demand for labor curve to the left
   d. increases the supply of labor

3. A rise in the tax on labor income:

   a. increases the real wage paid to labor
   b. has no effect on the after-tax wage paid to labor
   c. lowers the demand for labor
   d. lowers the willingness of labor to work

4. A rise in the level of productive government activities:

   a. increases the demand for labor
   b. lowers the marginal product of labor
   c. lowers employment
   d. raises unemployment

5. An overgrown government is one in which:

   a. taxes collected are insufficient to pay for the level of government spending
   b. the distorting effect of the tax on labor shifts the demand for labor curve to the left
   c. the budget deficit rises each and every year
   d. labor taxes lower the supply of labor and thus lower the level of output and employment

6. Supply-side policies include:

   a. controlling the money supply so as to keep inflation as close to zero as possible
   b. elimination of the government deficit
   c. lowering tax rates so that output rises and the aggregate supply curve shifts to the right

d. redistributing income from lower paid to higher paid workers

7. The Reagan administration's supply-side policies include:

   a. tax cuts and deregulation
   b. tight monetary policy
   c. a rise in national defense spending and the embargo on grain sales to the Soviet Union
   d. lobbying for larger quotas on beef and orange exports to Japan

<u>True or False</u>

1. A rise in the level of productive government activities paid for by an increase in the tax on labor income raises the demand for labor by more than it lowers the supply of labor and so raises output and employment.

2. A rise in the level of productive government activities paid for by a tax on labor income shifts the aggregate supply curve to the right.

3. An overgrown government that cuts some of its unproductive services will lower employment and lower the inflation rate.

4. A supply-side policy is any government policy that lowers inflation and unemployment.

5. Supply-side policies are aimed at shifting the aggregate supply curve to the right.

6. Supply-side policies always have the bad side effect of raising the deficit.

<u>Fill in the Blanks</u>

1. Productive government activity shift the production function____________, so that the ____________ ____________ of ____________ rises and the demand for labor curve shifts to the ____________ .

2. Higher taxes on labor income shift the supply of labor curve to the ____________, ____________ the before-tax real income and ____________ the after-tax real income. The level of employment ____________ .

3. Efficient government raises output, employment, and the real wage because the provision of ____________ government activities raises the ____________ ____________ and shifts the ____________ for labor curve to the right. The taxes imposed to pay for the increased provision of productive activities shifts the ____________ of labor curve to the ____________ . This shift to the left is ____________ than the shift of the ____________ for labor curve to the right.

4. An overgrown government is one in which increased spending and increased taxes levied to pay for the larger government shift the supply of labor curve so far to the ___________ that ___________, ___________ and the after-tax real wage all fall.

5. The Reagan administration's supply-side policies include ___________ defense spending, ___________ spending on domestic programs, ___________ taxes and ___________ . The hoped-for effects of these supply-side policies are a rise in ___________ and ___________. These effects will occur in the ___________ ___________ but in the short term the federal budget deficit will ___________ .

Answers

Multiple Choice: 1 b 2 a 3 d 4 a 5 d 6 c 7 a
True or False: 1 T 2 T 3 F 4 F 5 T 6 F
Fill in the Blanks
1. upwards, marginal product, labor, right
2. left, raising, lowering, falls
3. productive, production function, demand, supply, left, smaller, demand
4. left, employment, output
5. increasing, cutting, cutting, deregulating, output, employment, long term, rise

CHAPTER 40

U.S. ECONOMIC LINKS WITH THE REST OF THE WORLD

This chapter introduces the next part of the book--the United States and the World Economy. By now you are familiar with:

(i) The questions that macroeconomics seeks to answer.
(ii) U.S. macroeconomic history since 1900 and the way in which the main macro variables are measured in the United States.
(iii) The definition of the business cycle and co-movements among the variables along the cycle.
(iv) The determination of output, employment, unemployment, the interest rate and the price level in a closed economy.
(v) The implications of the rational expectations theory for the formation and conduct of macroeconomic policy.
(vi) The determinants of the long-term trend in output.

In this final part of the book the macroeconomic models already studied are extended to the open economy so that you can understand what determines the state of the balance of payments and the value of the exchange rate and how shocks emanating in other countries affect the U.S. economy and how those in the United States affect the rest of the world. This brief chapter gets you started on that process by introducing the basic concepts and definitions.

When you have completed your study of this chapter you will:

(a) Know the definitions of the current account, the capital account, the official settlements account, and the balance of payments.
(b) Know the definitions of a foreign exchange rate, an effective exchange rate, a fixed exchange rate, a flexible exchange rate, and a managed floating exchange rate.

Chapter Summary

A. Definitions of the Balance of Payments

The current account is the account that records the values of current goods and services sold abroad, the purchases of goods and services from abroad, debt interest receipts and payments, and unilateral transfers received from and paid abroad.
The capital account records the receipts and payments between residents and non-residents arising from the issue of new debt or the retirement of old debt.
The official settlements account records the movements in gold and foreign currency reserves (adjusted by any official borrowing) resulting from the net of the balances on the current and capital accounts. By accounting convention it is measured as the negative of the sum of the current and capital account balances so that the sum of the balances on all three accounts is always zero.
The balance of payments is defined as the sum of the balances on the current and capital account or, equivalently, as the negative of the official settlements balance.

An effective exchange rate is an index representing the relative price between one national currency and an average of other currencies. The weights on other currencies in the average reflect the importance of each currency in the international trade of the country in question.

B. Exchange Rate Definitions

A foreign exchange rate is the relative price between two currencies.
A fixed exchange rate is one which takes on a value declared and maintained by the active intervention of the Fed.
A flexible exchange rate is an exchange rate, the value of which is determined purely by market forces, with no direct Fed intervention.
A managed floating exchange rate is one which is manipulated by the Fed, but not manipulated according to any preannounced rules.

Multiple Choice

1. The current account of the balance of payments shows:

   a. how much U.S. residents have loaned to the rest of the world
   b. the change in official reserves
   c. the difference between exports and imports
   d. the sum of the difference between exports and imports, net interest receipts, and unilateral transfers

2. Recorded as a capital receipt in the capital account of the balance of payments are:

   a. the sale of U.S. government bonds by Canadians to other Canadians in Canada
   b. loans made by U.S. banks located in Toronto to Toronto manufacturers
   c. gold purchases by the Fed
   d. the sale of bonds by the U.S. government to Canadian residents

3. The official settlements balance is:

   a. the sum of the capital and current account balances
   b. the negative of the sum of the capital and current account balances
   c. the change in the money supply
   d. always in deficit

4. The foreign exchange rate is:

   a. the price at which the gross domestic product of one country can be exchanged for that of another
   b. the price of one money (domestic) in terms of another money (foreign)
   c. the domestic price of imports
   d. the foreign price of exports

5. A fixed exchange rate is:

   a. established by market forces
   b. pegged by the Fed
   c. a commitment that can never be broken
   d. a lucky accident

6. A flexible exchange rate:

   a. occurs only when there are climatic fluctuations
   b. results from Fed intervention in the foreign exchange market
   c. is determined by market forces
   d. results from supply shocks

7. A managed floating exchange rate is:

   a. pegged by the Fed
   b. determined by market forces
   c. partially pegged by the Fed and partially determined by market forces
   d. established by the Fed and maintained at that level

True or False

1. Unilateral transfers from abroad do not represent the payment for goods and services and so are not part of the balance of payments.

2. Dividends and interest paid on foreign investment represent the return on capital and so are part of the capital account of the balance of payments.

3. If a Canadian resident bought an apartment in Florida using a U.S. bank loan negotiated in Miami and paid interest on the loan from income earned in the United States, none of these transactions would appear in the U.S. balance of payments accounts.

4. If the United States discovered massive gold deposits in Alaska that were mined and completely bought by the Fed, then U.S. gold and foreign exchange reserves would rise and there would be a surplus on the official settlements balance.

5. If the Fed stood ready to buy and sell U.S. dollars at $2 U.S. per £, the United States would have a managed floating exchange rate.

Fill in the Blanks

1. The biggest item on the receipts side of the current account of the balance of payments is ____________________.

2. The purchase by Canadians of oranges from Florida appears in the ____________ account of the balance of payments.

3. If the current account was in surplus by $1 million and the capital account in deficit by $2 million and if there were no errors and omissions the official settlements balance would be a ____________ of $____________ .

4. If the central bank has no foreign exchange reserves and never trades in the foreign exchange market, the exchange rate is ____________ .

5. If the price of the Canadian dollar changes from 80¢ U.S. to 75¢ U.S. the Canadian dollar has ____________ by ______%.

Problem

Using the following items, construct the Balance of Payments accounts of the hypothetical economy and answer the following questions:

	$
Capital Imports	4,000
Debt Interest Received from Abroad	800
Exports of Goods and Services	2,000
Capital Exports	3,600
Gifts Made to Foreigners	200
Imports of Goods and Services	2,500
Gifts Received from Foreigners	700
Rise in Gold and Foreign Exchange Reserves	800

(a) What is the Current Account Balance?
(b) What is the Capital Account Balance?
(c) What is the balance on the official settlements account?
(d) What is the magnitude of the "errors and omissions"?
(e) Does this economy have a flexible exchange rate?

Answers

Multiple Choice: 1 d 2 d 3 b 4 b 5 b 6 c 7 c
True or False: 1 F 2 F 3 T 4 F 5 T
Fill in the Blanks:
1. exports of goods and services
2. current
3. surplus, $1 million
4. flexible
5. depreciated, 6.25

Problem: (a) $800 (b) $400 (c) -$800 (d) -$400 (e) no

CHAPTER 41

THE BASIC MODEL OF THE BALANCE OF PAYMENTS AND THE EXCHANGE RATE

When you have completed this chapter of the book you will:

(a) Understand the connection between the money supply and the foreign exchange reserves.
(b) Understand the "law of one price": (1) purchasing power parity (PPP), and (2) interest rate parity (IRP).
(c) Understand how the balance of payments is determined when the exchange rate is fixed.
(d) Understand how the exchange rate is determined in a flexible exchange rate regime.
(e) Understand how the balance of payments and the exchange rate are linked in a managed floating regime.

Chapter Summary

A. Money Supply and Foreign Exchange Reserves

The money supply is, by definition, equal to the sum of foreign exchange reserves and domestic credit.

B. The "Law of One Price"

The law of one price asserts that arbitrage will reduce price differentials to the minimum consistent with transport costs, tariffs, and other physical barriers and impediments to trade.

The purchasing power parity theorem states that the price of a particular good in one country will be the same as the price in another country (when the prices are converted at the current exchange rate). This proposition does not strictly apply to price levels, since tariffs and transportation costs drive a wedge between price levels. However, it does apply to price changes expressed in percentage terms. That is, the percentage change in the price of some commodity in the United States will be equal to the percentage change of the price of the same commodity in Canada (say) plus the percentage rate of depreciation of the U.S. dollar in terms of the Canadian dollar.

The interest rate parity theorem is an application of the law of one price to asset markets. It states that the rate of interest in Canada will be equal to the rate of interest in the United States plus the expected rate of depreciation of the $C.

C. Determination of the Balance of Payments Under Fixed Exchange Rates

In an economy with a fixed exchange rate, the balance of payments (as a first approximation) is determined exclusively by the domestic credit policies of the Fed. If the Fed creates too much domestic credit, there will be a balance of payments deficit. If the Fed creates too little domestic credit, there will be a balance of payments surplus. The Fed can always achieve a zero balance by permitting exactly the right amount of domestic credit to be created.

D. Determination of the Exchange Rate Under a Flexible Exchange Rate Regime

When the exchange rate is flexible, the money supply and its growth rate are controllable by the Fed. Inflation is determined in such a case by exactly the same way as it is in a closed economy, by the rate of growth of the money supply. The exchange rate is determined by the differences in money supply growth rates and output growth rates between countries. Specifically, the exchange rate, being a price like any other price, is determined by supply and demand. Since the exchange rate is the relative price between two monies, it is determined by the relative supplies (stocks) of the two monies and the relative demands for them. There is a sense in which the exchange rate is unlike any other price in that its value depends directly on the relative monetary policies of the two countries.

E. Determination of the Balance of Payments and the Exchange Rate in a Managed Floating Regime

For a given foreign rate of inflation, the faster the growth rate of domestic credit, the greater will be the amount of exchange market pressure. Exchange market pressure must come out either in a depreciation of the currency or a loss of foreign exchange reserves. The Fed can select a policy that favors smoothing exchange rate adjustments by permitting reserves to take the strain, or it may select a policy which favors steady stock of foreign reserve by permitting the foreign exchange rate to take the strain. The Fed cannot choose both the exchange rate and the stock of foreign exchange reserves.

Multiple Choice

1. If a commercial bank makes $1 million worth of new loans to households and firms:

   a. the money supply rises by $1 million
   b. domestic credit rises by $1 million
   c. foreign exchange reserves fall by $1 million
   d. there would be a balance of payments deficit

2. If the price of a car in Canada rises by 5% and if the U.S. dollar is depreciating, car prices in the United States will rise by:

   a. less than 5%
   b. more than 5%
   c. exactly 5%
   d. sometimes more and sometimes less than 5%

3. If interest rates in Canada are 10% per annum and in the United States they are 12% per annum, the foreign exchange value of the U.S. dollar is:

   a. falling
   b. rising
   c. constant
   d. fluctuating about a constant average

4. When the exchange rate is fixed, a rise in the rate of domestic credit expansion will:

   a. improve the current account balance
   b. worsen the current account balance
   c. worsen the capital account balance
   d. create a rise in the official settlements balance deficit

5. When the exchange rate is fixed, the money supply is determined by:

   a. Fed policy
   b. the policies of foreign central banks
   c. the demand for money
   d. foreign exchange reserves and domestic credit

6. When the exchange rate is flexible:

   a. depreciation of the exchange rate causes inflation
   b. exchange rate fluctuations are caused by fluctuations in the difference between the growth rate of money in the domestic economy and the growth rate of money in the rest of the world
   c. exchange rate fluctuations are determined by fluctuations in tariffs
   d. exchange rate fluctuations are determined by fluctuations in harvests

<u>True or False</u>

1. The supply of money is identical to the sum of notes and coins in circulation plus bank deposits. It cannot therefore be the same thing as the stock of foreign exchange reserves plus the stock of domestic credit.

2. The domestic rate of inflation will, on the average, necessarily be the same as the world rate of inflation.

3. Canadian interest rates must always move in line with U.S. interest rates.

4. When the exchange rate is fixed, a rise in prices in the rest of the world will make domestic industries more competitive and will therefore lead to a rise in the current account surplus.

5. Under fixed exchange rates the official settlements balance can be whatever the Fed wants it to be--it simply has to adjust domestic credit in the appropriate way.

6. Under flexible exchange rates a rise in domestic credit will only cause a depreciation of the currency if foreign exchange reserves are constant.

7. A rise in the growth rate of domestic real income will lead to a rise in the rate of appreciation of the domestic currency (other things equal).

8. A depreciating currency does not cause inflation.

9. A country can have both stable prices and a stable foreign exchange rate if it follows the appropriate monetary policy.

Fill in the Blanks

1. If the volume of bank deposits is \$550, domestic credit held by the commercial banks \$500, the total money base \$400, monetary base held by the banks \$50, and domestic credit held by the Fed \$300, then the stock of foreign exchange reserves is ___________.

2. The price of a car in the United States in year 1 was \$5,000 and in year 2 it was \$5,250. In year 1 it cost \$1.20 Canadian to buy \$1 U.S. In year 2 it cost only \$1.188 Canadian to buy \$1 U.S. In year 1 the price of a car in Canada was ___________. In year 2 the price of a car in Canada was ___________.

3. The rate of interest in the United States is 10% per annum. The rate of interest in Canada is 12% per annum. The average expectation in the market is that the U.S. dollar will ___________ vis-à-vis the Canadian dollar by ______%.

4. When the growth rate of domestic credit rises either the balance of payments deficit ___________ and/or the currency of the country ___________.

5. The rate of change of the foreign exchange rate in a flexible exchange rate regime will equal the difference between the domestic and foreign growth rates of the ___________ and the domestic and foreign growth rates of ___________.

Answers

Multiple Choice: 1 b 2 b 3 a 4 d 5 c 6 b
True or False: 1 F 2 F 3 F 4 F 5 T 6 F 7 T 8 T 9 F
Fill in the Blanks:
1. \$100
2. \$6,000, \$6,237
3. depreciate, 2%
4. rises, depreciates
5. money supply, real income

CHAPTER 42

THE KEYNESIAN MODEL OF THE OPEN ECONOMY

When you have completed this chapter you will:

(a) Know how to derive the IS curve for an open economy.
(b) Know the definition of the BP curve.
(c) Know how to derive the BP curve.
(d) Understand what makes the IS, LM, and BP curves shift.
(e) Know how to determine the levels of output, interest rate and the balance of payments in a fixed exchange rate regime.
(f) Know how to determine the levels of output, interest rate and the exchange rate in a flexible exchange rate regime.

Chapter Summary

A. Derivation of the IS Curve for an Open Economy

The IS curve for an open economy shows the relationship between the rate of interest and level of income at which savings-plus-taxes-plus-imports equals investment-plus-government spending-plus-exports. It is steeper than the IS curve for a closed economy and intersects the latter at the real income level and interest rate at which imports equal exports.

B. Definition of the BP Curve

The BP curve shows the relationship between the rate of interest and level of real income at which the balance on the official settlements account is zero.

C. Derivation of the BP Curve

For a given real exchange rate (i.e., a given level of domestic and foreign prices and nominal exchange rate) and given level of world income, exports will be fixed. The capital account surplus depends upon the domestic rate of interest, and imports depend on domestic income. By finding the level of real income that generates an import volume equal to the exports-plus-capital account surplus generated by a given interest rate, it is possible to trace out the BP curve. The curve slopes upwards, except in the case of perfect capital mobility, in which case it is horizontal.

D. Shifts in the IS, LM, and BP Curves

In addition to the factors that shift the IS curve in a closed economy, a change in world real income, the exchange rate, or the foreign price level shifts the IS curve in an open economy. A rise in world real income, a rise in the world price level, or a depreciation of the domestic currency shifts the IS curve to the right.

The LM curve shifts because of changes in the money supply. In an open economy when the exchange rate is fixed, this occurs if the balance of payments is other than zero. The balance of payments surplus is associated with a rising money supply, the balance of payments deficit with a falling money supply. Thus, if the economy is off the BP curve, the LM curve is shifting if the exchange rate is fixed.

The BP curve shifts as a result of changes in world real income, the exchange rate, the world price level, or the world rate of interest. A rise in world real income, a rise in the world price level, a fall in the world rate of interest, or depreciation of the currency shifts the BP curve to the right. A change in world income that shifts both the IS and the BP curves shifts both curves in the same direction but shifts the BP curve by more than it shifts the IS curve. A change in the real exchange rate also shifts both the IS and BP curves and we have assumed that the BP curve shifts by more than the IS curve.

E. Determination of Output, Interest Rate, and the Balance of Payments in a Fixed Exchange Rate Regime

At each instant, the real income level and interest rate are determined at the point of intersection of the IS and LM curves. If that intersection point is off the BP curve, the LM curve is shifting. The steady state occurs where the IS and BP curves intersect. The LM curve intersects this point as a result of the money supply adjusting while the balance of payments is out of equilibrium.

Expansionary fiscal policy raises output and interest rates and leads to a temporary balance of payments surplus. Expansionary monetary policy leads to a temporary balance of payments deficit and no steady-state change in real income or the rate of interest. A devaluation initially raises the rate of interest and real income level, but eventually lowers the rate of interest below its initial level and raises real income still further. In the process, the balance of payments will have been in surplus. A rise in world real income has a similar effect to that of a devaluation.

F. Determination of Output, Interest Rate, and the Exchange Rate in a Flexible Exchange Rate Regime

Under flexible exchange rates, the LM curve is fixed in position. The positions of the BP and IS curves depend on the value of the exchange rate. As the exchange rate varies, these curves shift to intersect each other along a downward-sloping IS-BP locus. The equilibrium exchange rate is the exchange rate which locates the BP and IS curves at an intersection point along the LM curve. In a flexible exchange rate economy, an expansionary fiscal policy raises real income and the rate of interest and appreciates the currency. An expansionary monetary policy lowers the rate of interest, raises the level of real income, and depreciates the currency. An expansion in world real income leads to an appreciation of the currency but no change in real income or the rate of interest.

Multiple Choice

1. The open economy IS curve traces the relationship between the rate of interest and the level of real income such that:

    a. investment equals savings
    b. government spending minus taxes plus exports minus imports plus investment minus savings equals zero

c. investment plus taxes equals saving plus government spending
d. investment plus taxes plus imports equals savings plus government spending plus exports

2. At all points above the BP curve there is:

   a. a balance of payments surplus
   b. a balance of payments deficit
   c. a balance of payments equilibrium
   d. no way of determining whether there is a balance of payments surplus or deficit

3. A rise in world real income will shift to the right:

   a. the IS curve only
   b. the BP curve only
   c. the LM curve only
   d. both the IS and the BP curves

4. Under a fixed exchange rate with a fixed price level, with income less than its full-employment level and with perfect capital mobility, a rise in government expenditure will:

   a. raise the rate of interest
   b. raise domestic credit
   c. raise the money supply
   d. generate a balance of payments deficit

5. Under flexible exchange rates with a fixed price level, with income less than its full-employment level and with perfect capital mobility, a rise in the money supply will:

   a. lower the stock of foreign exchange reserves
   b. lower interest rates
   c. depreciate the currency
   d. leave real income unchanged

6. Under a flexible exchange rate with a fixed price level, with income at less than its full-employment level and with perfect capital mobility, a rise in the foreign price level will:

   a. raise the domestic price level
   b. raise real income
   c. raise the money supply
   d. lower the foreign exchange rate

<u>True or False</u>

1. The IS curve in the open economy is less steep than in the closed economy.

2. The BP curve is steeper the lower the degree of international capital mobility.

3. Under flexible exchange rates the LM curve is irrelevant for determining the steady-state values of the rate of interest and the level of income.

4. When there is a rise in the world price level or world real income the IS curve and the BP curve shift to the right but the BP curve shifts by more than the IS curve.

5. A rise in the money supply under fixed exchange rates permanently raises aggregate demand.

6. Under flexible exchange rates a rise in government spending causes a depreciation of the currency.

7. A rise in the world price level has a bigger effect on domestic output under fixed exchange rates than under flexible rates.

8. A rise in the foreign rate of interest will lower real income under fixed exchange rates but raise real income under flexible rates.

Fill in the Blanks

1. Under fixed exchange rates with a fixed price level and income at less than its full-employment level, a rise in government spending will ____________ real income, ____________ the rate of interest, ____________ the money supply, ____________ the balance of payments.

2. Under fixed exchange rates with a fixed price level and income at less than its full-employment level, a rise in domestic credit has the following effects on the steady-state values: It ________________ real income, ________________ the rate of interest, ________________ the money supply, and ________________ the balance of payments.

3. Under fixed exchange rates with a fixed price level and income at less than its full-employment level, a rise in domestic credit will have the following impact effects: It ____________ real income, ____________ the rate of interest, ____________ the money supply, and ____________ the balance of payments.

4. Under fixed exchange rates with a fixed price level and income at less than its full-employment level, a rise in the foreign price level will ____________ real income, ____________ the rate of interest, ________________ the money supply, and ________________ the balance of payments.

5. Under flexible exchange rates with a fixed price level and income at less than its full-employment level, a rise in government spending will ____________ real income, ____________ the rate of interest, ________________ the money supply, and ________________ the balance of payments.

6. Under flexible exchange rates with a fixed price level and income at less than its full-employment level, a rise in domestic credit will

   ________________ real income, ___________ the rate of interest,

   ________________ the money supply, and ________________ the balance of payments.

7. Under flexible exchange rates with a fixed price level and income at less than its full-employment level, a rise in the foreign price level

   will ________________ real income, ___________ the rate of interest,

   ________________ the money supply, and ________________ the balance of payments.

Answers

Multiple Choice: 1 d 2 a 3 d 4 c 5 c 6 d
True or False: 1 F 2 T 3 T 4 T 5 F 6 F 7 T 8 T
Fill in the Blanks
1. raise, raise, raise, lower
2. leaves unchanged, leaves unchanged, leaves unchanged, leaves unchanged
3. raises, lowers, lowers, raises
4. raise, lower, raise, raise
5. raise, raise, leave unchanged, leave unchanged
6. raise, lower, raise, leave unchanged
7. leave unchanged, lower, leave unchanged, leave unchanged

CHAPTER 43

THE RATIONAL EXPECTATIONS THEORY OF THE OPEN ECONOMY: A SELECTIVE SKETCH

When you have completed your study of this chapter you will:

(a) Understand the need for a rational expectations theory of the open economy.
(b) Understand the implications of the assumption of perfect capital mobility for the determination of aggregate demand.
(c) Understand how output and the price level are determined with perfect capital mobility, rational expectations, and a fixed exchange rate.
(d) Understand how output, the price level, and the exchange rate are determined with perfect capital mobility and rational expectations in a flexible exchange rate regime.

Chapter Summary

A. The Need for a Rational Expectations Theory of the Open Economy

The need for a rational expectations theory of the open economy arises from the same considerations as in the case of the closed economy. The basic model accounts for some facts, and the Keynesian model for others, but neither accounts for all the facts. The rational expectations theory, which emphasizes the distinction between anticipated and unanticipated shocks, offers, in effect, a method of combining the best of both of these models into a single unified framework. There is a clear need to extend that framework to handle the determination of output and prices as well as the exchange rate and balance of payments in an open economy.

B. Aggregate Demand when Capital is Perfectly Mobile

If capital is perfectly mobile, the rate of interest is determined exogenously in the rest of the world. In a fixed exchange rate economy, aggregate demand is determined purely by the IS curve and the world rate of interest. Shifts in aggregate demand therefore depend on changes in the world price level, world real income, world interest rate and domestic fiscal policy. In a flexible exchange rate world, aggregate demand is determined solely by the domestic demand for money, supply of money, and the world interest rate. Changes in aggregate demand in that case depend only on the world rate of interest and the money supply. In a fixed exchange rate setting, the LM curve determines the money supply via the balance of payments; and in the flexible exchange rate setting, the IS curve determines the real and nominal exchange rates.

C. Determination of Output and Price Level with a Fixed Exchange Rate

The expected values of fiscal variables and foreign variables determine the expected aggregate demand curve, which in turn determines the rational expectation of the price level. The actual aggregate demand curve intersecting the expectations-augmented aggregate supply curve determines actual output and prices. Anticipated changes in fiscal policy or foreign variables will have price level effects only; unanticipated changes will affect both output and the price level. Fluctuations in the current account of the balance of payments will be countercyclical. Domestic output will be procyclical with world output. An anticipated foreign inflation or depreciation of the currency will raise the price level proportionately.

D. Determination of Output, the Price Level, and the Exchange Rate Under Flexible Exchange Rates

With flexible exchange rates, the continuous information given by the exchange rate has to be used to form a rational expectation of the shocks influencing the economy. If there was one, and only one, source of shock, then knowledge of the exchange rate would enable a perfect inference to be made and would ensure that the economy always operates at full-employment equilibrium. The effects of all shocks in that case would be exactly the same as in the basic model.

If there is more than one source of shock (for example, a money supply and a real exchange rate shock), then observation of the (nominal) exchange rate alone does not enable a complete identification to be made concerning the magnitude of those shocks. In general, an unexpected rise in the money stock will be associated with an unexpected drop in the real exchange rate and vice versa. That is, at least two expectational errors will be made that offset each other and give rise to an expectation of the exchange rate that is the same as the actual exchange rate.

An actual rise in the RE curve, with no change in the money stock, will, in general, be partly misinterpreted as a smaller rise in the RE curve than has actually occurred, accompanied by a rise in the money stock. Its effect will be to lower output, raise the price level, raise the real exchange rate, and depreciate the currency. The current account of the balance of payments will move into a bigger surplus or smaller deficit since the fall in income and rise in the real exchange rate will lower imports and raise exports. A rise in the money supply, which raises the exchange rate, will partly be interpreted as a rise in the real exchange rate. Its effect will be to raise output, the price level, the nominal exchange rate, and the real exchange rate. Its effect on the current account will be ambiguous since the higher real income level will raise imports, but the higher real exchange rate will have an offsetting effect on imports and will stimulate exports.

Multiple Choice

1. When capital is perfectly mobile internationally and the exchange rate is fixed, aggregate demand depends on:

    a. domestic monetary and fiscal policy
    b. domestic monetary policy, the world price level, the world interest rate, and the world real income
    c. domestic monetary policy and the world interest rate
    d. domestic fiscal policy, the exchange rate, the world price level, the world interest rate, and the world real income

2. When capital is perfectly mobile internationally and the exchange rate is flexible, aggregate demand depends on:

   a. domestic monetary and fiscal policy
   b. domestic monetary policy, the world price level, the world interest rate, and world real income
   c. domestic monetary policy and the world interest rate
   d. domestic fiscal policy, the exchange rate, the world price level, the world interest rate, and world real income

3. a. If the exchange rate is flexible, aggregate demand is determined by the intersection of IS and BP curves, the LM curve adjusts automatically
   b. If the exchange rate is fixed, aggregate demand is determined by the intersection of the LM and BP curves, the IS curve adjusts automatically
   c. If the exchange rate is flexible, aggregate demand is determined by the intersection of IS and LM curves, the BP curve adjusts automatically
   d. If the exchange rate is flexible, the real exchange rate is determined by the variables which are exogenous to the IS curve, namely world interest rates, world real income, and domestic fiscal policy variables

4. In a fixed exchange rate regime when capital is perfectly mobile internationally:

   a. the expected price level will be revised only when the expected money supply or the expected world interest rate changes
   b. an unanticipated rise in world interest rates raises domestic prices and output
   c. an anticipated rise in domestic fiscal policy raises domestic output
   d. the real exchange rate is constant

5. In a fixed exchange rate regime with capital perfectly mobile internationally:

   a. a negative aggregate supply shock raises the real exchange rate and deteriorates the balance on the current account
   b. a positive aggregate demand shock raises the price level and output, lowers the real exchange rate and so the current account improves and the capital account worsens
   c. anticipated depreciation of the exchange rate by 10% raises the price level by 10% and does not change the current account balance
   d. an anticipated rise in the world interest rate raises aggregate demand, raises the domestic price level and lowers the real exchange rate

6. In a flexible exchange rate world with capital perfectly mobile internationally:

   a. a positive aggregate demand shock leads to a surprise depreciation of the exchange rate. If agents interpret the surprise as arising from an aggregate demand shock, then there will be an upward revision of the expectation of the price level
   b. a positive aggregate demand shock which leads to a surprise rise in the exchange rate which is interpreted as a real exchange rate shock will lead to a downward revision of the real exchange rate
   c. a positive real exchange rate shock interpreted as an aggregate demand shock leads to a rise in the exchange rate and a rise in the real exchange rate but to no change in the price level
   d. a positive real exchange rate shock interpreted as a real exchange rate shock leads to no change in the exchange rate but to a rise in the real exchange rate and the price level by the same amount

<u>True or False</u>

1. An unanticipated rise in aggregate demand in the rest of the world will have no effect on the output of a small open economy facing perfect capital mobility provided that the exchange rate is flexible.

2. An anticipated rise in world interest rates when capital is perfectly mobile internationally could either raise or lower the domestic price level.

3. If capital is perfectly mobile internationally and exchange rates are flexible an anticipated expansion of fiscal policy does not raise the domestic price level, domestic inflation or the domestic interest rate.

4. If capital is perfectly mobile internationally and exchange rates are fixed an anticipated expansion of government spending leads to a higher price level, a depreciated exchange rate, and higher inflation.

5. An anticipated devaluation when capital is perfectly mobile internationally raises the domestic price level and leaves domestic interest rates and output unchanged.

6. The effect of an unanticipated domestic monetary shock when exchange rates are flexible leads to a rise in the exchange rate, the price level and the real exchange rate as well as a rise in output.

7. Expansionary monetary policy in a fixed exchange rate world when capital is perfectly mobile has no effect on domestic price level or inflation rate or output. It purely lowers the stock of foreign reserves.

8. An unanticipated rise in the real exchange rate when nominal exchange rates are flexible leads to actual output and the price level being less than expected and the actual real exchange rate being above that expected. These errors "cancel out" so that the observed value of the exchange rate is also that expected.

Fill in the Blanks

1. When capital is perfectly mobile internationally, the domestic interest rate __________ the world interest rate, and a rise in the value of the exchange rate shifts the _____ curve but not the _____ and _____ curves.

2. In a world where capital is perfectly mobile, an unanticipated devaluation __________ the price level, __________ output, __________ the current account balance and __________ the capital account balance.

3. A surprise drop in the terms of trade when the exchange rate is flexible, __________ the price level, __________ output, and __________ the exchange rate.

4. An anticipated rise in foreign interest rates __________ the price level and __________ the exchange rate if exchange rates are flexible but __________ the price level if exchange rates are fixed.

5. Anticipated expansionary monetary policy has only one effect on the economy. If the exchange rate is flexible, it ____________________. If the exchange rate is fixed, it ____________________.

Answers

Multiple Choice: 1 d 2 c 3 d 4 b 5 c 6 a
True or False: 1 F 2 T 3 T 4 F 5 T 6 T 7 T 8 T
Fill in the Blanks:
1. equals, IS, BP and LM
2. raises, raises, worsens, improves
3. raises, lowers, raises
4. raises, raises, lowers
5. depreciates the exchange rate, reduces the stock of foreign reserves

CHAPTER 44

THE U.S. ECONOMY AND THE REST OF THE WORLD

When you have completed your study of this chapter you will:

(a) Know the main patterns of world output, prices, interest rates, and exchange rates in the 1970s.
(b) Understand the causes of world output, prices, interest rate and exchange rate movements in that period.
(c) Understand how the United States has influenced the world economy in the 1970s.
(d) Understand the policy choices facing the United States in its relations with the rest of the world.

Chapter Summary

A. The Main Patterns of World Output, Prices, Interest Rates, and Exchange Rates in the 1970s

World output growth went into a boom in 1972-1973 and a deep recession in 1974-75. It recovered in 1976, but trended downward slightly towards the end of the 1970s.

World inflation exploded in 1973-1974, moderated markedly in 1975-1976, but then accelerated again towards the end of the decade. Interest rates followed the inflation pattern very closely. The U.S. dollar was fairly steady against the Canadian dollar, depreciated slightly against the Deutsche mark and the yen, and appreciated against the British pound in the first half of the 1970s. It depreciated substantially against all major currencies except the Canadian dollar in the second half of the 1970s. Growth rates in output have been remarkably similar in all countries throughout the 1970s, whereas inflation and interest rates have diverged markedly, especially after 1974.

B. The Causes of World Output, Price, Interest Rate and Exchange Rate Movements in the 1970s

The macroeconomic theory of the closed economy may be used to understand the movements of world average output and prices. Although in principle, world aggregate fiscal policy variables play a role, it turns out that movements in world money supply growth are quite capable of explaining the main trends in both output and inflation. It is necessary to interpret there as being about a two-year lag before money growth is fully incorporated into inflation in the first half of the decade, and approximately a one-year time lag in the second half of the decade. The divergence of inflation and interest rates across the major countries in the second half of the decade is seen as arising from the pursuit of diverging monetary policies in a world of flexible exchange rates.

C. How the United States Has Influenced World Macroeconomic Developments in the Postwar Period

Under both the fixed exchange rate era (World War II to early 1970s) and the floating exchange rate era (the 1970s up to date), U.S. macroeconomic developments have had a major influence on the rest of the world.

With fixed exchange rates, countries necessarily found themselves linked to U.S. macroeconomic fortunes. Stimulation in the United States automatically led to stimulation elsewhere as countries sought to prevent their foreign exchange reserves from rising too quickly. Conversely, deflationary pressures in the United States led to deflationary pressures elsewhere as countries sought to protect their foreign exchange reserves.

In the floating exchange rate era, an unwillingness to see exchange rates move too quickly has led countries to continue synchronizing their monetary policies with those of the United States, although in the latest U.S. deflation, less than completely so.

D. Macroeconomic Policy Choices

The United States has more macroeconomic policy freedom than other countries. Although it cannot impose a fixed exchange rate system on the rest of the world, it can nevertheless pursue whatever monetary policies it chooses regardless of whether the world operates on fixed or floating exchange rates. Other countries have less freedom of choice. At the extremes, a small country may choose a flexible exchange rate with monetary targeting, or it can choose a fixed exchange rate, with the money supply and inflation being determined by the country (or countries) against whom the exchange rate is fixed. In the present state of knowledge, we cannot say definitively which one of the extremes is better than the other. It is possible to say, however, that world inflation may be avoided by firm domestic monetary policies that are pursued with long-term credibility. This requires that exchange rates be flexible.

Multiple Choice

1. The growth rates of aggregate output in the United States, Canada, the Big Seven, and the OECD in the 1970s have:

   a. been uncorrelated with each other
   b. systematically declined
   c. shared a common cyclical pattern
   d. demonstrated that the United States has the highest average growth rate in the industrial world

2. The inflation rate in the United States, Canada, Japan, Germany, the United Kingdom, and the world as a whole, in the 1970s:

   a. share a common cyclical pattern
   b. have systematically increased
   c. show that U.S. inflation is the worst in the world
   d. have become increasingly divergent

3. Interest rates in the major countries during the 1970s:

   a. were highest in those countries whose inflation was highest
   b. were essentially equal
   c. shared a common cyclical pattern but had different average levels
   d. became more similar in the later years of the decade

4. The massive explosion of inflation in 1973-4 was:

   a. accompanied by a massive explosion in the growth rate of the money supply
   b. preceded by a massive explosion in the growth rate of the money supply
   c. followed by a massive explosion in the growth rate of the money supply
   d. completely unrelated to the growth rate of the money supply

5. Under the Bretton Woods international monetary system the United States:

   a. could choose the exchange rates between the U.S. dollar and all other currencies
   b. stood ready to buy and sell U.S. dollars so as to maintain its exchange rate
   c. could pursue whatever monetary policy it chose without having any effect on other economies
   d. could pursue any monetary policy it chose but as U.S. monetary policy induced changes in the stocks of foreign reserves in other countries so U.S. monetary policy was transmitted to other countries

6. The U.S. economy under floating exchange rates:

   a. had no influence on the macroeconomic developments in the rest of the world
   b. was more affected than the rest of the world by the oil shock of 1973
   c. was beset by problems of its own but it had no effect on the rest of the world
   d. was heavily influenced by macroeconomic developments in the rest of the world

7. The lesson that we learn from macroeconomic theory and U.S. macroeconomic history in the 1970s is that:

   a. it is easy for a country to insulate its domestic economy from U.S. economic influences by adopting a flexible exchange rate
   b. domestic policy errors are the major macroeconomic problem
   c. it is very hard for the rest of the world to insulate against U.S. output fluctuations
   d. fixed exchange rates are better than flexible exchange rates

<u>True or False</u>

1. The United States suffered a bigger decline in output following the first oil shock (1974-5) than any other major country.

2. U.S. inflation went up higher and came down faster than that in any other country.

3. The U.S. dollar lost value against all the major currencies during the 1970s.

4. Interest rates in Canada and the United States trended upwards throughout the 1970s whereas in Japan and Germany they rose sharply in the middle 1970s but thereafter declined.

5. The world business cycle in the 1970s cannot be accounted for by fluctuations in the growth rate of the world money supply.

6. The time lags between changes in the growth rate of the world money supply and changes in the growth rate of world output lengthened during the 1970s.

7. The timing and the cross-country evidence on money supply growth and oil price changes show, unambiguously, that world inflation was caused by the oil price rise and not by monetary expansion.

8. Thanks to flexible exchange rates the United States has achieved a great deal of independence and so influences the world macroeconomy less in recent years.

Fill in the Blanks

1. The world business cycle in the 1970s saw output growth rates rising from 1970 to ____________, declining from ____________ to ____________, rising again from ____________ to ____________ and then declining.

2. The peak inflation of the 1970s occurred in all the major countries in ____________ with the exception of ____________ where inflation peaked in ____________. Following that peak, inflation fell but the country experiencing the most dramatic fall was ____________.

3. In 1970, the spread between the highest inflation rate, that of ____________ and the lowest, that of ____________ was ____________%. By 1979 the spread between the highest inflation rate, that of ____________ and the lowest, that of ____________, had become ____________%.

4. Following the oil price rise in 1973 inflation increased in Japan to ____________% and in Germany to ____________%. This suggests that the oil shock ____________ the major cause of the worldwide inflation explosion of the middle 1970s.

Answers

Multiple Choice: 1 c 2 d 3 a 4 b 5 d 6 d 7 c
True or False: 1 T 2 F 3 F 4 T 5 F 6 F 7 F 8 F
Fill in the Blanks:
1. 1973, 1973, 1975, 1975, 1976
2. 1974, the United Kingdom, 1975, Japan
3. Japan, Germany, 4, the United Kingdom, Japan, 9
4. 25, 7, was not

[illegible]

6. The [illegible] lines [illegible] the [illegible] should [illegible]
readily and [illegible]

[illegible]